To Alex and Isy — RP

First edition for the United States, its territories
and dependencies, and Canada published in 2014
by Barron's Educational Series, Inc.

Text, design, and illustration © copyright 2014
by Carlton Books Ltd.

All inquiries should be addressed to:
Barron's Educational Series, Inc.
250 Wireless Boulevard
Hauppauge, NY 11788
www.barronseduc.com

ISBN: 978-1-4380-0557-7

Library of Congress Control Number: 2014932008

Date of Manufacture: June 2014
Manufactured by: R.R. Donnelley & Sons, Dongguan, China

Product conforms to all applicable CPSC and CPSIA 2008
standards. No lead or phthalate hazard.

Printed in China
9 8 7 6 5 4 3 2 1

Editors—Barry Timms and Anna Brett
Art Editor—Emily Clarke
Designer—Amy Clarke
Illustrations—Melissa Four
Publisher—Sam Sweeney
Creative Director—Clare Baggaley
Consultant—Holly Cave
Picture Research—Ben White
Production—Ena Matagic

Produced under license from SCMG Enterprises Ltd.
Science Museum ®SCMG.
www.sciencemuseum.org.uk

The Science Museum, London, is the U.K.'s most popular
destination dedicated to science, technology, engineering,
medicine, design, and enterprise, and is an internationally
renowned visitor attraction. As the home of public
engagement with science, we combine our unparalleled
collection of historical objects with cutting-edge technology
and contemporary science news and debate, to help our
visitors make sense of the science that shapes their lives and
to inspire the next generation of scientists.

Author Acknowledgments

Thanks to Jacob Watson for his
advice at the book's planning stage.

Picture Credits

The publishers would like to thank the following sources
for their kind permission to reproduce the pictures in
this book.

Key, T=top, L=left, R=right, C=center, B=bottom

Alamy: Dinodia Photos: 90l
Bridgeman Art Library: /British Library Board: 117b
Corbis: /Auslöser: 96br, /Mark Thiessen/National Geographic
Society: 27c, /Peyton Williams/Icon SMI: 131r, /Jim Smithson:
134l, /Tanner Productions: 85r
David Trood: The Face of Humanity: 55l, 55c
Getty Images: 46br, 50tr, 50cl, 50cr, 52 (all celebrity pics),
61br, 95tl, 95c, 95bl, 136br, /Barcroft Media: 139br, /Chaos:
102b, /Don Farrall: 40c, /FilmMagic: 50tl, 50bl, /Franklin
Lugenbeel: 131l, /Radius Images: 133b, /Gabrielle Revere:
49tr, /Philip and Karen Smith Philip and Karen Smith: 59b,
60, /WireImage: 49c, 50br,
Science Photo Library: /Life In View: 136l, /Dr. G. Moscoso:
105tr, /Dr. Gopal Murti: 132br /D.Phillips: 104

All other images: iStockphoto.com, Shutterstock.com,
Thinkstockphoto.co.uk

Every effort has been made to acknowledge correctly and
contact the source and/or copyright holder of each picture.
Carlton Books Limited apologizes for any unintentional
errors or omissions, which will be corrected in future
editions of this book.

SCIENCE MUSEUM

THE ULTIMATE BOOK ABOUT

RICHARD PLATT

BARRON'S

CONTENTS

So what's actually in this book?

WHAT DOES IT MEAN TO BE "ME?"

"WHO ARE YOU?"
Most of us answer this question with our names, without really thinking. However, a name doesn't say much about who we really are.

For instance, it doesn't reveal:

- what we look like
- how good we are at remembering things
- the color of our hair
- how fast we can run
- how healthy we are
- what scares us
- all our happiest memories

And yet all these things—and many more—are essential ingredients in the recipe that make each of us who we are. So what really does give us our identity?

The answer is more complex—and more interesting and more amazing—than any name.

9

IDENTITY

Much of our identity comes from our genes: biological plans that help decide how our bodies develop and grow. Our genes are so compact that 4,000 complete sets of them would take up no more room than a grain of salt. Yet each complete set contains enough data to fill a CD.

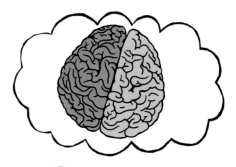

The other important part of your identity is in your brain. Though it looks like little more than a fragile blob of gray jelly, your brain is amazingly complex and clever. It controls your movement. It creates and processes your thoughts. It gives you the ability to see, hear, and talk—and to love and hate. And it stores your every memory.

This book is about these two extraordinary things: your genes and your brain. So turn the page, and find out who you are, and what makes you unique and different from everyone else.

THE PRACTICAL STUFF

Finding your way around a long book can be a challenge, but there are some helpful clues if you know where to look.

MY GENES

• At the top of every left-hand page you'll find a label that shows which section you're in.

• Words in *italics*, or sloping letters, are explained at the back of the book in the glossary.

All the information needed to make you unique is contained in your *genes*, which are contained in your *DNA* in packages called *chromosomes*.

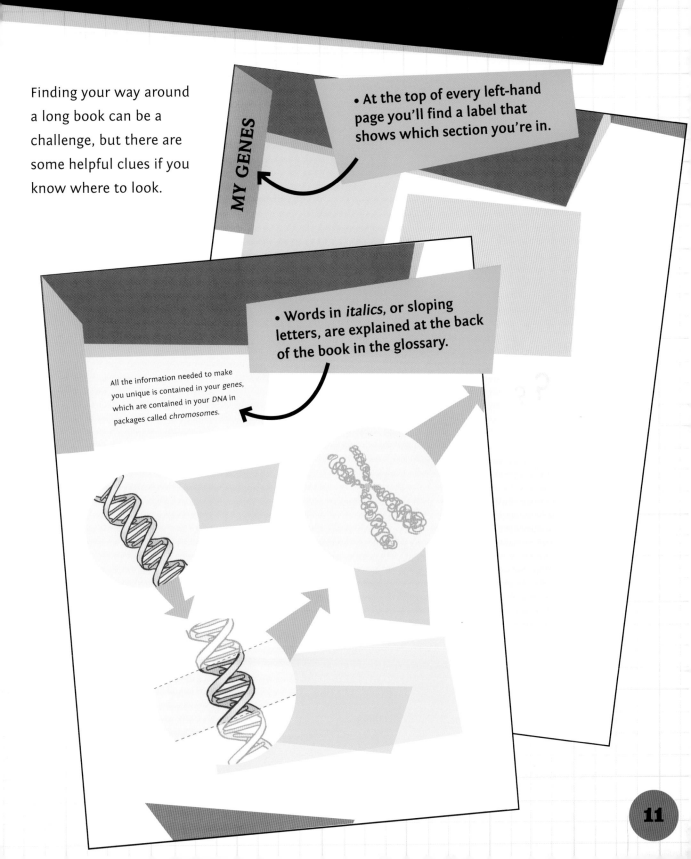

AM I REALLY UNIQUE?

YES!

You are absolutely, completely, and utterly YOU. There never has been, and never will be, anyone quite like you anywhere in the world!

Q SO WHAT EXACTLY MAKES ME UNIQUE?

A One major factor is your genes: a complex set of biological instructions, like the plans of a building. Genes guide your growth and development by helping to make proteins—the building blocks of your body. They do this from the time you were a single cell through your whole lifetime, right up until your death. Half of your genes come from your father and half from your mother.

Two strands of DNA are wound around each other to form a twisted ladder called a "double helix."

The rungs of this ladder are actually a sequence of special chemicals called "base pairs." This sequence is different in everybody, and forms the genetic code that makes you who you are.

Q WHERE ARE MY GENES?

A They are in most of the cells in your body. Genes are sections of DNA—a chemical like a long, twisted ladder—and are made from some three billion "base pairs." It's the arrangement of these within the genes that makes each of us different.

Q HOW SMALL IS A GENE?

A Human genes vary greatly in size, but a typical gene is about $^1/_{1000}$ of a millimeter in length—that's very small! The DNA containing the genes comes in packages called "chromosomes." If one of these was stretched out to form a thin thread, it would be about 2 in. (5 cm) long.

Q BUT I HAVE AN IDENTICAL TWIN WHO LOOKS JUST LIKE ME...

A "Identical" twins share the same genes, but they are still not exactly the same. Even before birth, they experienced tiny differences that affected their development. Try this: you and your twin brother each press the same finger on a rubber-stamp ink pad, then on a sheet of white paper. Examine them closely with a magnifying glass—they are not identical!

(Darn! There go your chances of committing the perfect crime and blaming your brother!)

Q WOULD MY CLONE BE EXACTLY LIKE ME?

A Cloning makes a copy of a living thing with exactly the same genes. In a laboratory, it's possible to clone animals—and probably people, too. It's done by removing the DNA from an animal's egg, replacing it with the DNA from the adult to be cloned, then growing the egg inside a host mother. Twins are natural clones, and artificial human clones would be just as similar—though they would be different ages.

Er, hello, nice to meet me!

INSTRUCTIONS FOR MAKING YOU

All the information needed to make you unique is contained in your *genes*, which are contained in your *DNA* in packages called *chromosomes*.

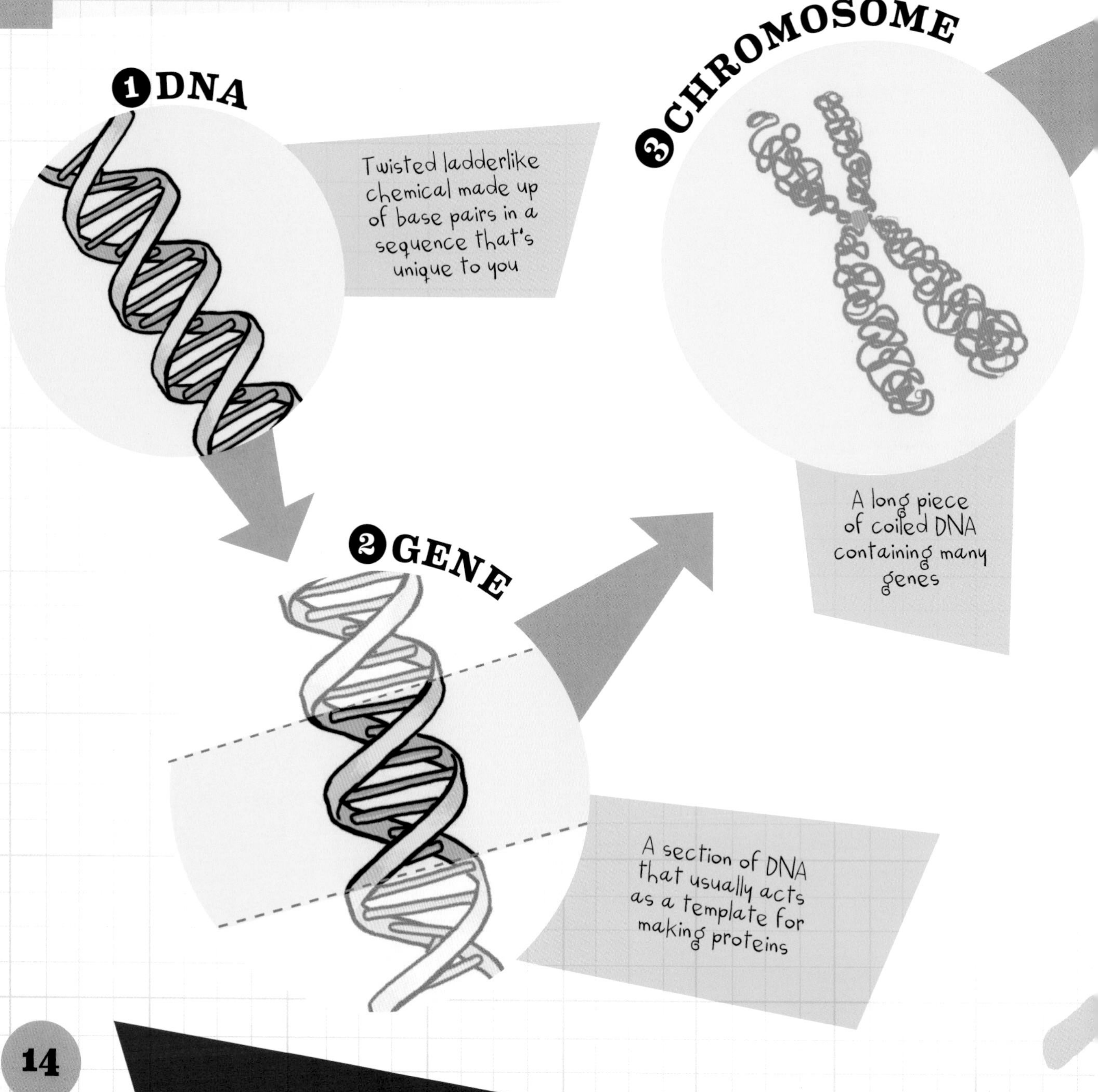

❶ DNA

Twisted ladderlike chemical made up of base pairs in a sequence that's unique to you

❸ CHROMOSOME

A long piece of coiled DNA containing many genes

❷ GENE

A section of DNA that usually acts as a template for making proteins

❹ NUCLEUS

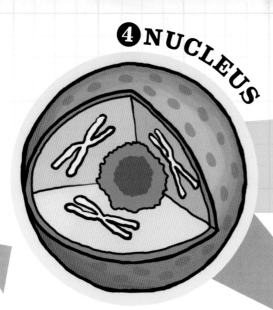

The central part of most human cells, containing your 46 chromosomes

❺ CELL

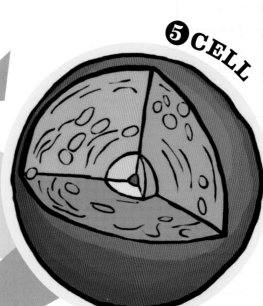

The smallest living part of the human body

YOU!

You're made of some 100 trillion cells!

WHAT'S SO SPECIAL ABOUT GENES?

You would be amazed at the range of different things about you that genes control.

As well as the immediately obvious things like gender, height, and hair color...

WHAT ELSE?

Whether you have the potential to be an Olympian or a gourmet chef...

In fact, genes affect many things about you, from the biggest, like your gender, to the tiniest, weirdest details.

KEEP ON RUNNING
Want to know if you'll ever be an Olympic champ? A gene test could provide a clue. Top athletes tend to have an unusual *variant* of the ACTN3 "sprint" gene—those without seem to have slightly weaker muscles. Unfortunately, *inherit*ing the right genes from your parents isn't enough on its own to make you a winner. Training plays a much bigger part.

WEIRDEST GENE OF ALL?

Do you like asparagus? Have you noticed that after eating this weird pointy green vegetable, your urine smells weird, too? Maybe not: some people can't detect the odor at all. You genetically inherit this ability to smell "asparagus urine," so if one of your parents can smell it, you probably can too.

HAVEN'T YOU GROWN!

Genes affect many different things about your body, from hair and eye color to height. However, there's rarely just one gene in control. Usually, many are involved in deciding each detail of what you look like and how you behave. Your *environment* and health make a difference, too. For example, many genes affect your height. If you have two tall parents, the genes you *inherit* from them will make you more likely to grow tall. But if you have a poor *diet*, or if your parents smoke, you may be no taller than any of your classmates.

WHY DO I LOOK LIKE MY GRANDMA BUT NOT MY MOM?

We all get it: "Don't you look like your mom?" or "You've got your dad's eyes." What's odd, though, is that some of us look more like our grandparents than our parents. Why? Genes are the reason. They pass on family stuff from parents to children, but they mix it up on the way.

WHERE DID YOU GET THOSE GENES?

Chromosomes in father's ordinary body cells

 1

1 Within our *DNA*, *genes* are arranged in packages called *chromosomes*. Everybody has two complete sets of 23 chromosomes in most of their *cells*, like two suits of playing cards. They got one chromosome in every pair from each of their parents. Here, we'll concentrate on the father's DNA.

2

Chromosomes in father's sperm

2 To make children, the body forms special sex cells—men make *sperm cells* and women make *egg cells*. These special cells contain only one copy of each chromosome. The copy that is chosen from mom or dad is a random process.

3

Baby's chromosomes from father's sperm   Baby's chromosomes from mother's egg

3 When a man and a woman try to have a baby, a sperm cell and an egg cell merge and make one new cell. Once again, this contains two sets of all 23 chromosomes—one copy from the man and one copy from the woman. The cell grows into a baby, who has a *random* mix of the parent's genes.

So what about the grandma thing?

Genes can appear to "skip" a generation because sometimes they can be hidden by other stronger genes.

HERE'S HOW IT WORKS...

Mom's mom had red hair, but her dad is dark. His dark-hair version of the hair-color gene is stronger than grandma's red, so Mom has dark hair.

Dad's dad has red hair, too, but his wife's stronger dark-hair version of the gene ensures that Dad has dark hair, too.

However, kids inherit half the genes of each parent, so although Mom has dark hair, she carries the red-hair gene. Dad also carries one red-hair version of the gene, even though his own hair is not red.

WHAT? SO HOW COME MY HAIR IS GINGER?!

To have red hair, you need two red-head versions of the hair-color gene. Since your mom and dad both have one, and kids inherit half of each parent's genes, they have a one in four chance of having a child with red hair.

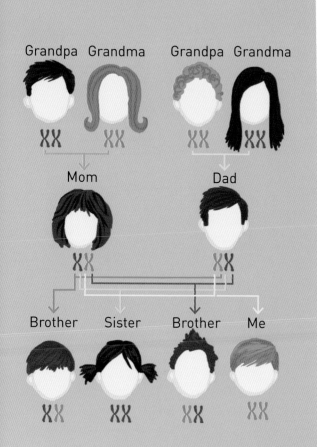

Grandpa Grandma   Grandpa Grandma

XX   XX   XX   XX

Mom   Dad

XX   XX

Brother   Sister   Brother   Me

XX   XX   XX   XX

HOW DO GENES SHAPE MY BODY AND MY LIFE?

Are you a boy or a girl?
It's in your *genes*.
What color are your eyes?
You get that from your genes, too.

What color is your hair?
Is your earwax runny or flaky?

WHAT!?

Yes, what kind of earwax you have is also controlled by your genes.

Take a look at some of the other things your genes determine.

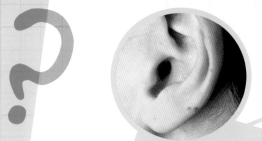

WHAT'S THIS EAR?
Flappy or attached earlobes run in families.

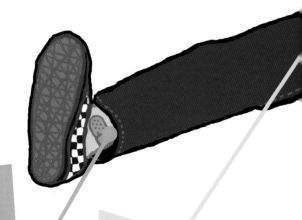

CURSE OR CURE?
People noticed centuries ago that whole families suffered from certain rare diseases, such as hemophilia (bleeding that won't stop). We now know that these are just the most obvious examples of "*genetic disorders.*" Genes also play a silent part in nearly 200 illnesses, some of them very common. A growing understanding of genetics is helping researchers predict who will fall ill, and to find cures.

FACE THE FACTS
Parents can pass on to their children their face freckles—along with their pale skin.

NEED A LIFT?
A *gene* controls whether or not you have a "hitchhiker's thumb" that bends back very far.

JUST CAN'T STOP MYSELF
Addicts have cravings so strong that they just can't get enough of a drug. Tobacco, alcohol, and other drugs light up the "mental reward" circuits of our brains, and genes can make addiction more likely. People with an uncommon form of the CHRNA5 gene, for example, get a bigger buzz from tobacco. This is not all bad news—this information could help scientists to find a way for smokers to quit.

WHO ATTRACTS YOU?
Most adults form relationships with people of the opposite gender, but about one in every ten find their own gender more attractive. Genes may have something to do with this. Studies of gay men who have gay brothers, uncles, or cousins suggest that some of them share the same unusual pattern on one particular gene.

SO IS EVERYTHING ABOUT ME DECIDED BEFORE I AM BORN?

If genes are so important, then what can I do to change my life? Whether I will succeed or fail, whether I'll be happy, even what I'll die of—all these things were decided before I was even born!

Yes, but what about brain stuff? Smart parents have smart kids, right?

Okay, but the kid in our class who always scores best in math tests has a professor for a mom and a best-selling author for a dad.

Yes, but you're just saying that to make me work harder. You can't prove that it's his hard work rather than his genes that make it easier for him to get "A"s in everything.

So are you saying that I won't grow up to be as bossy as you and as irritable as Dad?

Huh! You really think that would make me a happier person?

Well, hold on! Genes are only part of the story. You might have a gene that makes you more likely to suffer from a disease, but that doesn't mean you're DOOMED. Even if your genes make you vulnerable to lung cancer, you probably won't die from it unless you smoke.

Well, there's a lot more to how well you do in school than just which genes you've got.

They probably also make sure he studies, and help him a lot.

No, I can't. But you can study identical *twins* separated as babies and raised very differently. They have the same genes, and their intelligence is similar, but they often turn out to have very different behavior and personalities.

That's right. Genes do affect what you grow up to be, but your experience influences you, too. And a very useful experience for you right now would be to go and clean your room.

Maybe not, but it would make ME happier!

23

HOW WELL DO I KNOW MY BODY?

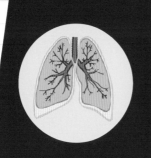

1. SPREAD OUT FLAT, THE SURFACE OF MY LUNGS WOULD COVER THE AREA OF...

A. this book
B. a table
C. seven parking spaces

2. MY BODY REMEMBERS THE IDENTITY OF EVERY GERM THAT HAS INFECTED ME...

A. in the last month
B. in the last year
C. forever

3. MY BODY'S ARTERIES AND VEINS ARE LONG ENOUGH TO STRETCH...

A. four times around a bus
B. three times the length of a football field
C. two-and-a-half times around the Earth

4. THE BIGGEST ORGAN IN MY BODY IS...

A. my skin
B. my heart
C. my liver

QUIZ TIME!

5. DURING EACH DAY I...

A. grow by a third of an inch (1 cm)
B. shrink by half an inch (1.25 cm)
C. stay the same height

6. SMOKING A PACK OF CIGARETTES A DAY MAKES DEATH FROM LUNG CANCER...

A. twice as likely
B. five times more likely
C. 25 times more likely

7. MY BODY PRODUCES AS MUCH HEAT AS...

A. a small flashlight
B. a standard lightbulb
C. an electric fire

8. MY EYE CAN RECOGNIZE...

A. one thousand different colors
B. ten thousand different colors
C. millions of different colors

How did you do? Find out the answers on page 26.

QUIZ ANSWERS

1. ANSWER: C
Your *lungs* are vast, because they require a large surface area to allow for large quantities of oxygen to be absorbed from the air. The oxygen passes through the skin of your lungs and into your blood.

2. ANSWER: C
Your *immune system* records every germ you have ever met, so if you meet it again, you have strengthened defenses against infection.

3. ANSWER: C
Your body contains the most amazing network of blood pipes. Including the tiniest, they stretch for 60,000 miles.

4. ANSWER: A
Just like your heart and liver, your skin is an *organ*. As well as protecting you against infection, it controls your temperature and makes vitamins that are essential to your health.

5. ANSWER: B
Measure yourself! Gravity compresses the spongy discs between your spine bones when you stand, but they expand by the same amount each night.

6. ANSWER: C
It may be legal, but tobacco is the deadliest drug available. It kills nine times as many people as heroin and cocaine put together.

7. ANSWER: B
Sitting still, you produce about 100W—as much as an old-fashioned lightbulb. Exercise makes you much hotter, though.

8. ANSWER: C
More than on any paint chart, though we can't name them all! However, one in every ten men is color blind and can't tell the difference between red and green.

At your fingertips?
The end of your nose?

Don't be so sure!

People who lose limbs in accidents soon get to feel that the artificial replacements are really part of their own bodies.

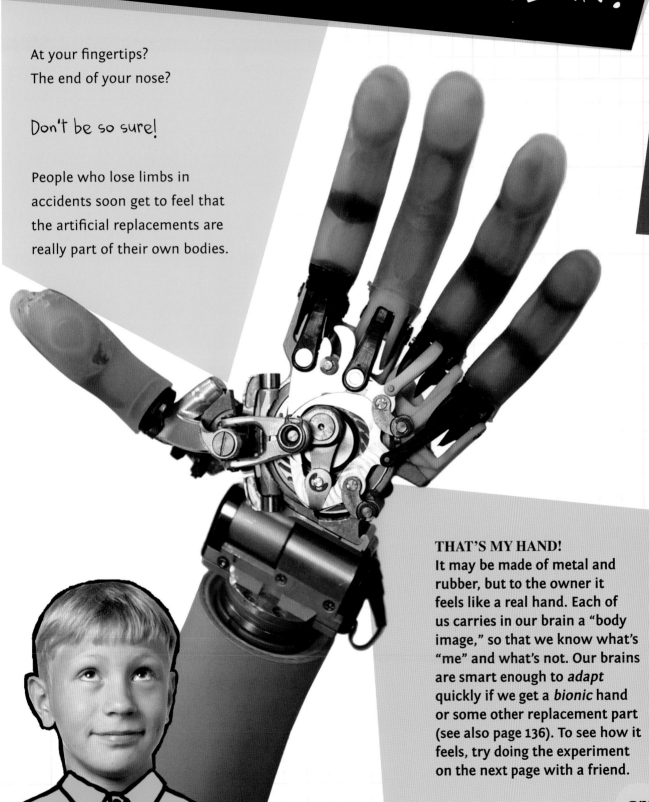

THAT'S MY HAND!
It may be made of metal and rubber, but to the owner it feels like a real hand. Each of us carries in our brain a "body image," so that we know what's "me" and what's not. Our brains are smart enough to *adapt* quickly if we get a *bionic* hand or some other replacement part (see also page 136). To see how it feels, try doing the experiment on the next page with a friend.

WOULD MY BODY FEEL "MINE" IF I HAD AN ARTIFICIAL LIMB?

YOU WILL NEED:

- a big cardboard box
- two paintbrushes
- a towel
- a rubber glove stuffed with paper to look like a hand
- a plastic ruler

Experiment TIME!

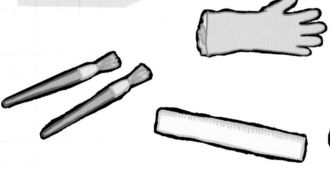

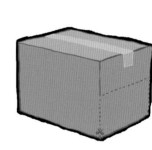

Method

1 Ask your friend to sit at a table and place his or her left forearm through the hole in the box as shown, so that he or she can no longer see it.

2 Put the stuffed glove on the other side of the box so that your friend can see it. Then arrange the towel to "join" it to your friend's left shoulder, forming an imaginary arm.

3 Now take the brushes and stroke the fingers of the real hand and the rubber hand at the same time, brushing the same finger on each and using the same rhythm. Continue for a minute or so, then slap the rubber hand with the ruler. (Make sure you don't hit the real hand!)

Results

Did your friend jump, as if the rubber hand was his or her own?

OUCH!

Conclusion

This "alien hand" illusion is convincing because our senses work together. During the experiment, your friend used his or her sense of vision, touch, and *proprioception* (the feeling of where the limbs were positioned). Because the brush touched the same parts of the real and fake hand, he or she was fooled into feeling that the glove had become part of his or her own body.

WHY ARE WE ALL DIFFERENT SHAPES AND SIZES?

Pause for a moment in a crowded street, and look at the people around you. Our bodies come in an astonishing range of different heights and widths. There's no Human Being: Standard Model. But why? What makes us the shapes and sizes we are? *Diet* and exercise have something to do with it, but *genes* play a major part, too.

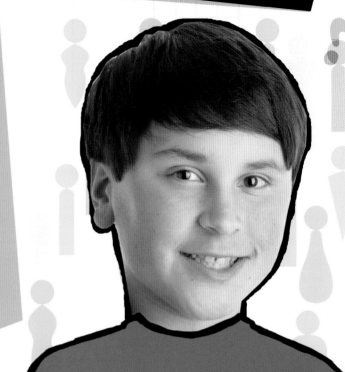

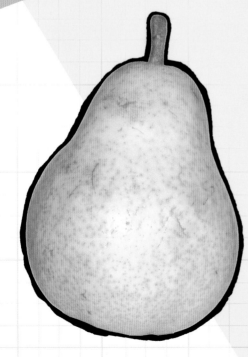

MOST OF US WILL END UP LOOKING LIKE OUR PARENTS

It's true: each of us *inherit*s our basic body shape, or "*physique,*" from our mother and father. Just as our *genes* affect our height, so they also influence our overall shape and size. If your mom and dad tend to store fat around their middles—a "pear" body shape—then the chances are you will, too.

AVERAGE IS BIGGER THAN YOU THINK

Most people are not built like sticks or balloons. The *average* person's figure is slightly plump. For women, that means dress size 16. Don't believe it? Count clothes on a rack. Wider waists outnumber narrow ones. Clothes shops don't stock what they can't sell, and the smallest sizes fit very few people.

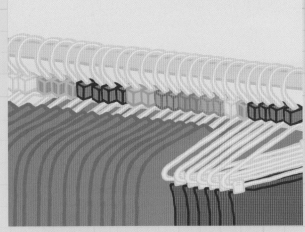

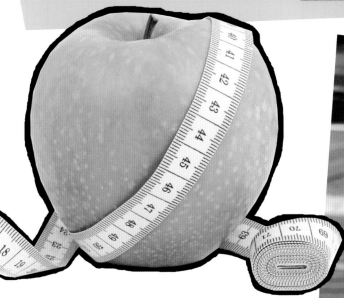

AIMING FOR MEDIUM

Exercise and *diet* really can reshape our bodies. In the right combination, they tighten up or build up *muscle*, and give us fuller or slimmer figures. However, strange and short-term diets don't make lasting changes. To stay at a steady, healthy weight, you need to always eat sensible amounts and get *vigorous* exercise several times every week.

HOW MANY? WHAT SIZE?

If you made a crowd of people stand in rows according to their sizes, the chart below shows how long the rows would be. Hardly anybody would be in the super-skinny row or in the super-sized row. Most would have a Body Mass Index of between 22 and 30.

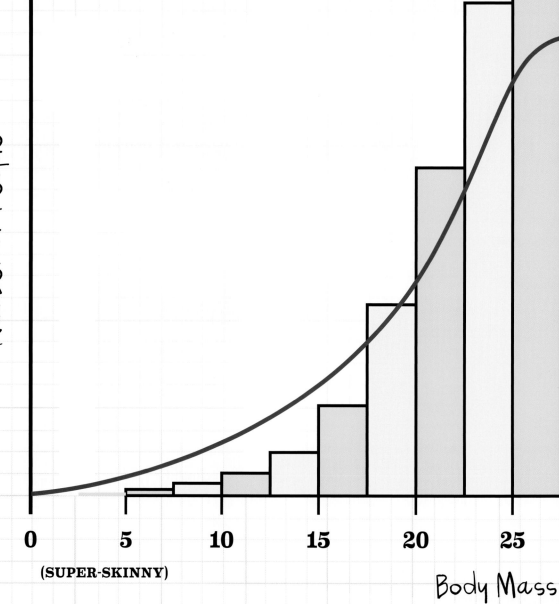

Number of People

0   5   10   15   20   25

(SUPER-SKINNY)

Body Mass

COMPARING SIZES

Body Mass Index (BMI) measures whether people are healthy weights for their heights. To work out your own BMI, do this...

1   **Weigh yourself in pounds (or kilograms)**

2   **Divide this by your height in feet (or meters)**

3   **Divide the result by your height again**

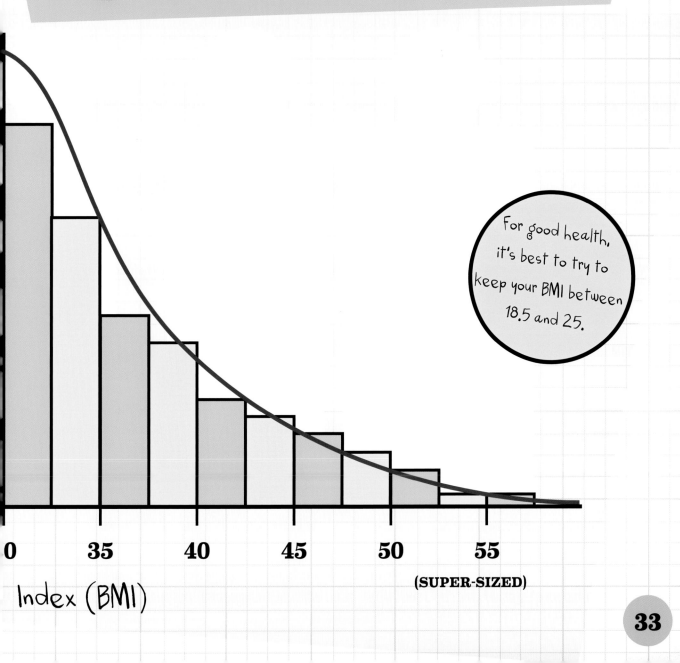

For good health, it's best to try to keep your BMI between 18.5 and 25.

0   35   40   45   50   55

(SUPER-SIZED)

Index (BMI)

IS MY BRAIN JUST A WET COMPUTER?

Fortunately, your brain is a little more reliable than that, or you might see a message like this one.

!

Application "GoToSchool" v3.1 has a fatal exception error. Unfortunately, this also caused thinking, breathing, and heartbeat to stop. Please report this error to the life-support team.

What's my brain like?

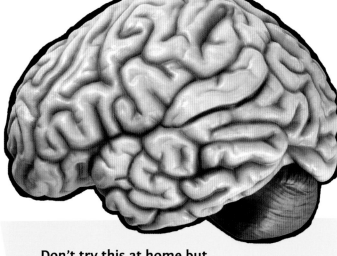

Don't try this at home but ... if you saw off the top of your head and lift out your brain, you would see that it is shaped like a big mushroom. It weighs about 3 pounds (1.4 kg) and has a surface wrinkled like a walnut. Prod it, and you'd find that your brain is very soft, like jelly. It's mostly an off-white color, tinted pink by the blood flowing through it.

Both gather information from different sources.

Both process the information.

Both store information for use later.

Both can control actions.

Both use electrical signals.

Both can work automatically.

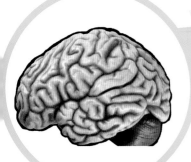

IT'S TRUE THAT BRAINS AND COMPUTERS DO **SIMILAR THINGS**

HOWEVER, THERE ARE ALSO MANY **DIFFERENCES**

BRAINS can (usually but not always) adapt and repair damage.

COMPUTER hardware cannot repair damage.

BRAINS are always at work—there's no "off" switch (until you die!).

You can turn a COMPUTER off.

BRAINS work using chemical changes as well as electrical pulses.

COMPUTERS only use electrical pulses.

BRAINS are much better at solving new or unexpected problems.

COMPUTERS are faster at routine tasks such as computation.

BRAINS create *emotions*, and can imagine, dream, and hope.

COMPUTERS can't imagine, dream, or hope—or experience any *emotions*.

WHAT EXACTLY DOES MY BRAIN DO?

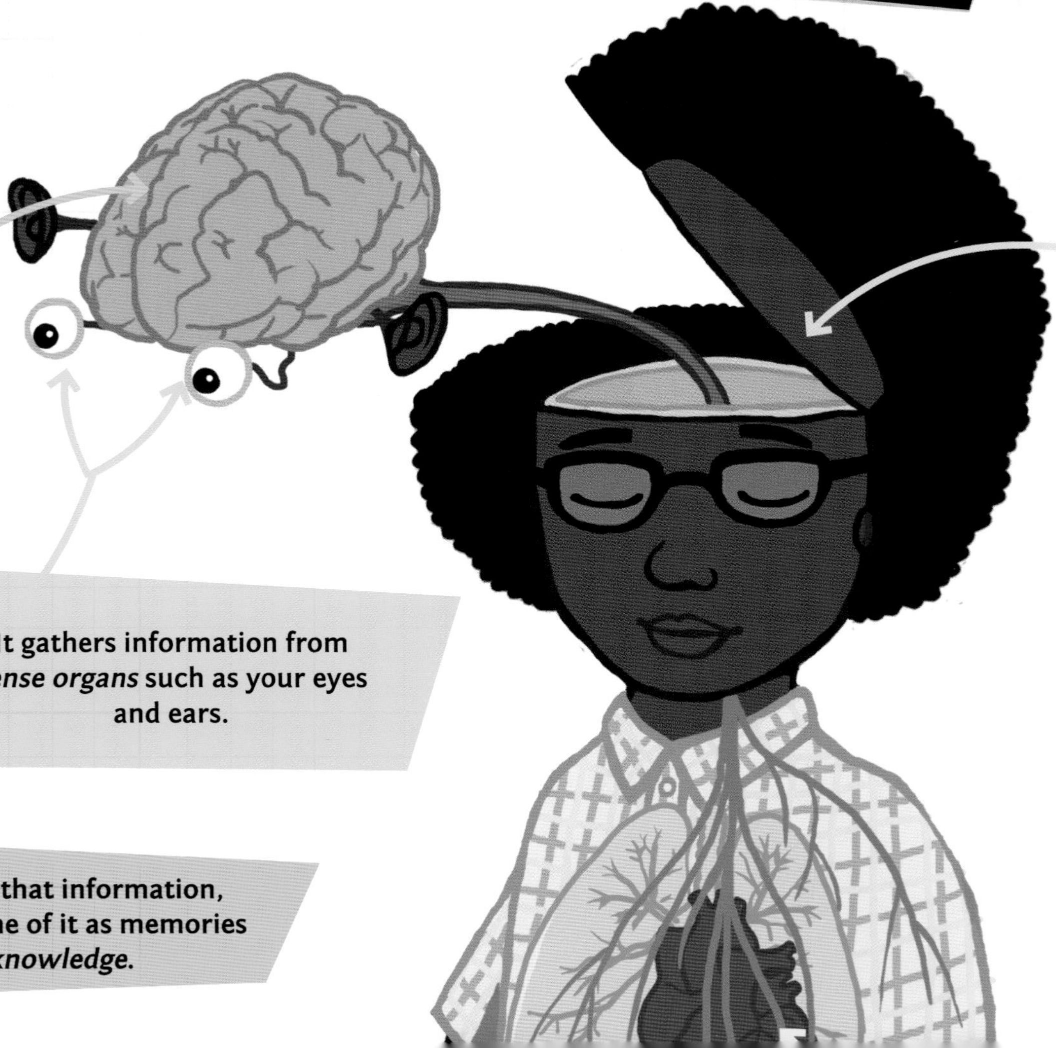

Protected inside the ball of bone that's your skull, the brain is your body's central control *organ*.

It gathers information from *sense organs* such as your eyes and ears.

It processes that information, recording some of it as memories and *knowledge*.

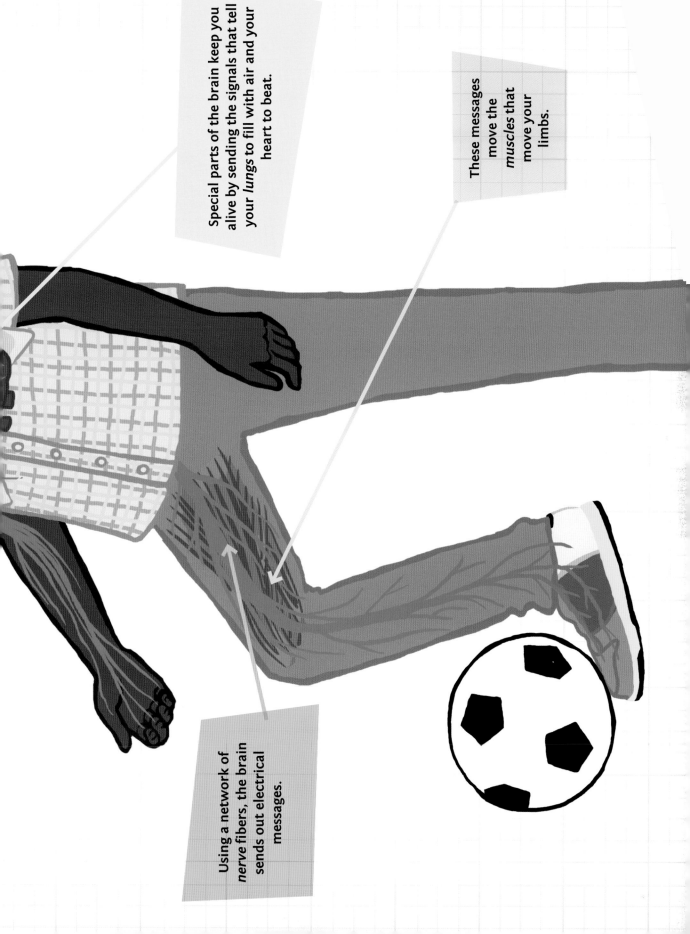

Special parts of the brain keep you alive by sending the signals that tell your *lungs* to fill with air and your heart to beat.

These messages move the *muscles* that move your limbs.

Using a network of *nerve* fibers, the brain sends out electrical messages.

HOW MANY BRAINS HAVE I GOT?

One, of course!
Or is it really two?

Your *cerebrum*—your brain's wrinkled, thinking top—has a great big gap splitting it into left and right sides. So, in some ways, you have two brains, not one. Each side has some unique jobs to do: the left brain, for example, controls your right limbs, and vice versa. Scientists think that each half-brain may work harder at certain different tasks, some of which you can see in the diagram on the right. But for much more of your thinking, feeling, and reacting, they share the work between them.

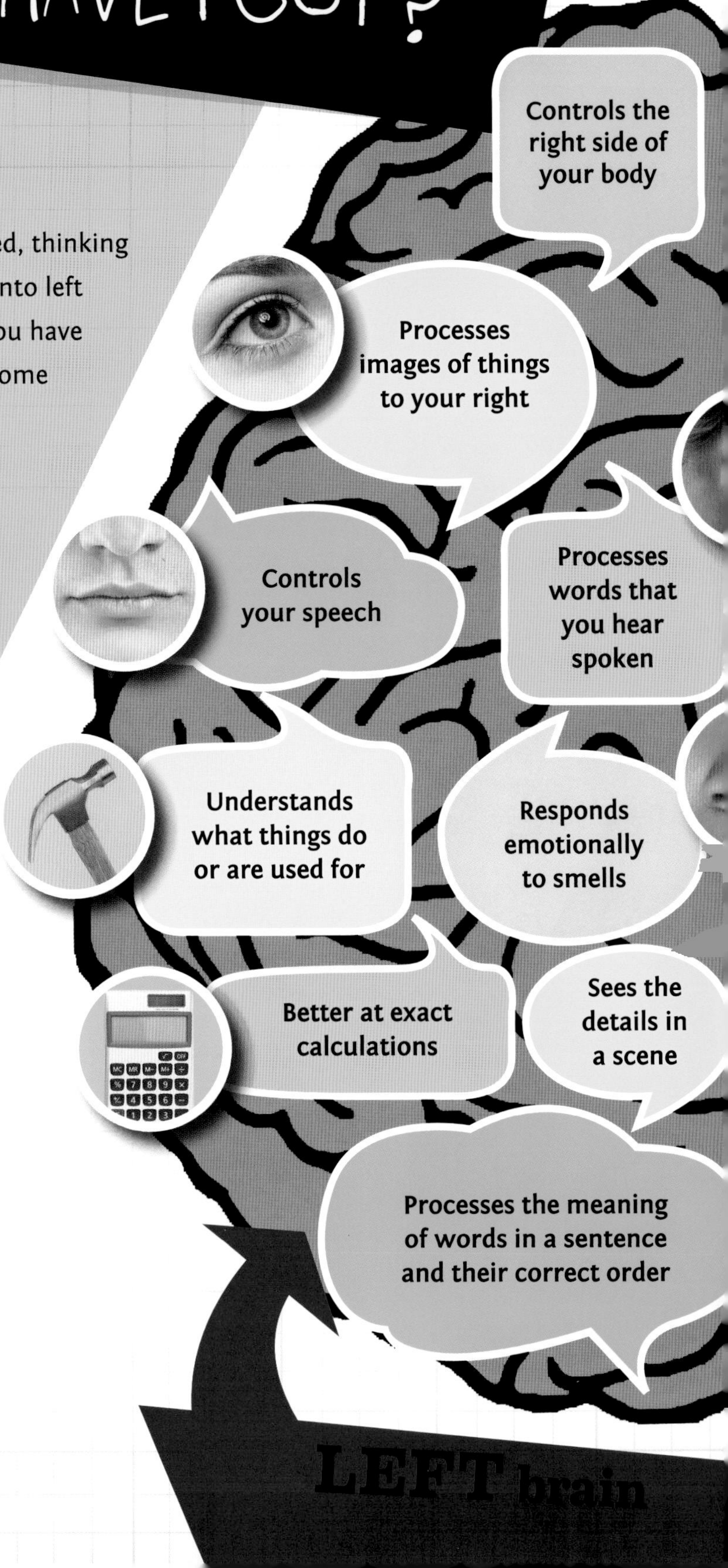

Controls the right side of your body

Processes images of things to your right

Controls your speech

Processes words that you hear spoken

Understands what things do or are used for

Responds emotionally to smells

Better at exact calculations

Sees the details in a scene

Processes the meaning of words in a sentence and their correct order

LEFT brain

HOW DO WE KNOW WHICH SIDE DOES WHAT?

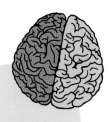

Controls the left side of your body

To learn about the brain's two halves, scientists first studied people who had injured one side of their heads to see what tasks they could and couldn't do. The information gained from brain scans now helps with this research.

Processes images of things to your left

Ahh, that explains why I am so smart!

Processes music that you hear

Understands words but cannot talk about them

Recognizes and identifies smells

Processes what things look like

Sees the big picture

Better at rough estimates

Understands word jokes such as puns, and processes the emphasis and tone in a sentence

RIGHT brain

39

WHICH PART OF THE BRAIN DOES WHAT?

Brain scans are a picture of a cross-section of the living brain.

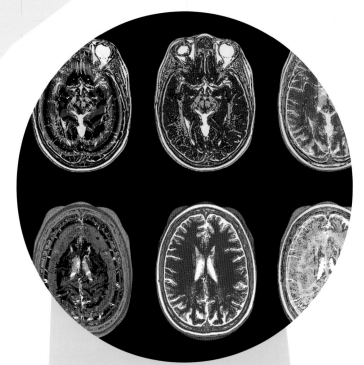

Recently, brain scans have allowed us to look inside the skull. Scans can show up in vivid colors the activity taking place, so we can see which parts of the brain are busiest when we do different activities.

Where does anger come from?
Find out more on page 101.

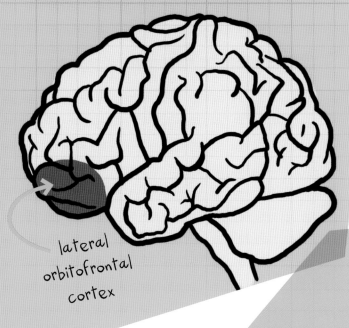

lateral
orbitofrontal
cortex

Find out MORE...

How do we smell?
Find out more on pages 63 and 72.

amygdala

hippocampus

olfactory bulbs

Control room of fear

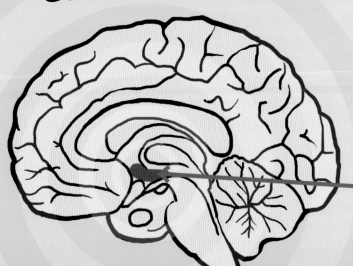

The centers of fear in the brain are the amygdalae. See page 91 for more!

amygdala

WILL MY BRAIN EVER RUN OUT OF SPACE?

We seem to collect more and more memories as we get older. It's amazing we don't need the mental equivalent of a hard-disc upgrade when we hit our twenties!

So how is there room in my head for ALL THIS STUFF?!

Fortunately, our brains are very *adaptable* because of the way they work. They can "rewire" themselves to make room for more *knowledge*, or to repair damage.

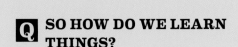

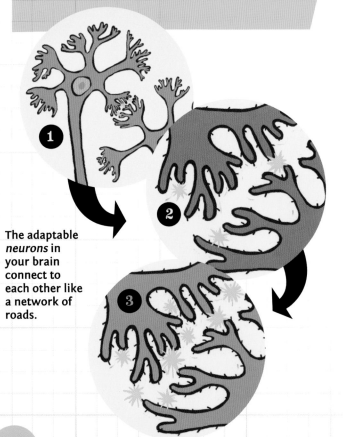

The adaptable *neurons* in your brain connect to each other like a network of roads.

Q SO HOW DO WE LEARN THINGS?

A By making links between *neurons*. These *nerve* fibers fill much of our brains.

1 Each grows links to other neurons around it.

2 Neurons talk to each other by "firing"—sending an electric pulse.

3 Anything we experience with our senses makes many neurons fire at the same moment. This strengthens the links among them. Having the same experience again makes links even stronger. That's why repeating things helps us to learn.

Q DO WE GROW MORE NEURONS AS WE AGE?

A No. By the time you can walk, you've got as many *neurons* as you are ever going to have. After the age of 20, they begin to die off.

Q DO SPARKS FLY BETWEEN NEURONS?

A Hardly. There's only about one tenth of a volt of power—that's 150 times weaker than the weakest flashlight battery.

! APPROACHING FORGETFUL ZONE

Q WHAT! I'LL GRADUALLY FORGET EVERYTHING I KNOW?

A No, your remaining *neurons* carry on making connections pretty much until you die.

Q SO THERE IS NO LIMIT TO THE NUMBER OF LINKS IN MY BRAIN?

A Nobody really knows, but an upper limit would explain why we can't remember stuff forever. It looks as though the links created by new learning wipe out some older, unused links.

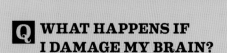

Q WHAT HAPPENS IF I DAMAGE MY BRAIN?

A A lot depends on which part is broken. *Knowledge* of an event is stored in many places in your brain, so a bump on the head won't make you forget everything. Your brain can even "rewire" after severe injuries. If you damage the part that controls your right hand, for example, nearby neurons might slowly take over control, so that you can grip again.

Q BUT ISN'T THAT A PROBLEM?

A Well, forgetting can be an advantage. Understanding what a lock does enables you to open any door for which you have a key. But you don't want to remember every detail of every door you open in your life.

WHAT DOES MY BRAIN DO WHEN I SLEEP?

We spend a third of our lives snoozing, yet the only thing scientists know for sure about sleep is that it stops us feeling tired! By wiring up sleepers' scalps, researchers have revealed how falling asleep changes waves of electrical energy in the brain. However, we still don't know why we sleep. Experts can't agree whether it rests and restores our brains, keeps us safe at night, saves our energy, or whether there's much more to it.

AWAKE

You are alert. Your brain is active and controls your body movements. You have vivid sensations created by your *sense organs*.

DREAMING SLEEP

You cannot move your body but your eyes dart quickly back and forth, which is why dreaming sleep is often called "rapid-eye-movement" or *REM sleep*. Your brain is even busier than when you are awake. Your experiences seem real, though they come not from your senses but from deep within your brain.

DOZING

You may be vaguely aware of your surroundings. You can still move your body a bit, though it sometimes jerks suddenly. Your eyes roll slowly. You wake easily.

LIGHT SLEEP

You're no longer conscious. Your eyes have almost stopped moving. You may move your body to stay comfortable, but you can't control these movements.

FAST ASLEEP

The deepest level of sleep: this is the time when you may walk or talk in your sleep, or have frightening sleep terrors.

Sleep phases

When you go to bed and doze off, you drift through several sleep stages, and you only dream in one of them. This sleep routine repeats itself several times each night.

I have loads more energy after a good sleep!

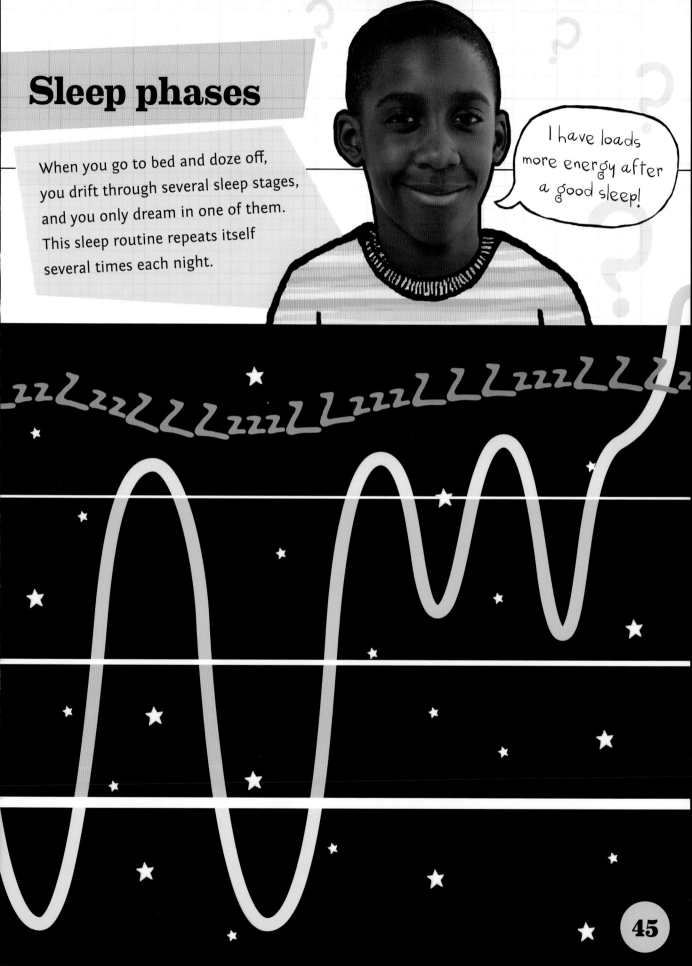

THE MYSTERY OF DREAMING

Nobody knows why we dream, or why dreams are so strange. One explanation is that dreaming helps us to learn and lay down memories. Processing the day's *knowledge* at night triggers random thoughts and sensations. Our dozy brains stitch them together into a weird story.

ZzZZ   ZZZzzzZzz

HOW MUCH SLEEP DO I NEED?

Enough to stop you feeling sleepy! Everybody is different. Some of us need ten hours; others manage with half of this. Teenagers often don't get enough sleep. Their *circadian rhythms* (brain clocks) are not regular, so they don't feel sleepy until very late at night.

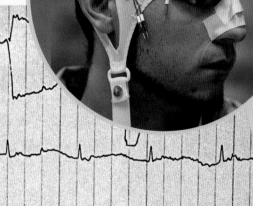

Amazing SLEEPY facts

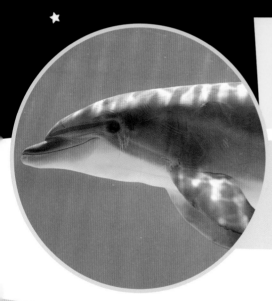

Bottlenose dolphins are always at least half awake—the left and right sides of their brains take turns snoozing.

Mammals and some birds are the only animals that dream.

STUDYING SLEEP
Sleep experiments are tough, because questioning a sleeper wakes them up. To learn about sleep, scientists measure the brain's electrical waves using an electroencephalograph (*EEG*). The wiggling lines change as we drift from dozing to sleeping to dreaming.

HOW DO OTHERS RECOGNIZE ME?

Even if you can't remember someone's name, there's a good chance that his or her face is familiar. That's because our brains are "wired" to deal with faces in a special way. A region of the brain called the fusiform face area works especially hard to try to remember who we are looking at when we see a face.

Weird FACE fact

Brain scans of car nuts and bird spotters show that when these experts look at the objects they love, they turn on the same parts of their brains that the rest of us use to recognize faces.

Vroom!

WHO'S THAT IN THE MIRROR?
About one in every 40 people suffers from mild *prosopagnosia*, or "face blindness." Very rarely, brain disease or damage stops people recognizing anyone, including members of their families—and their own faces in the mirror!

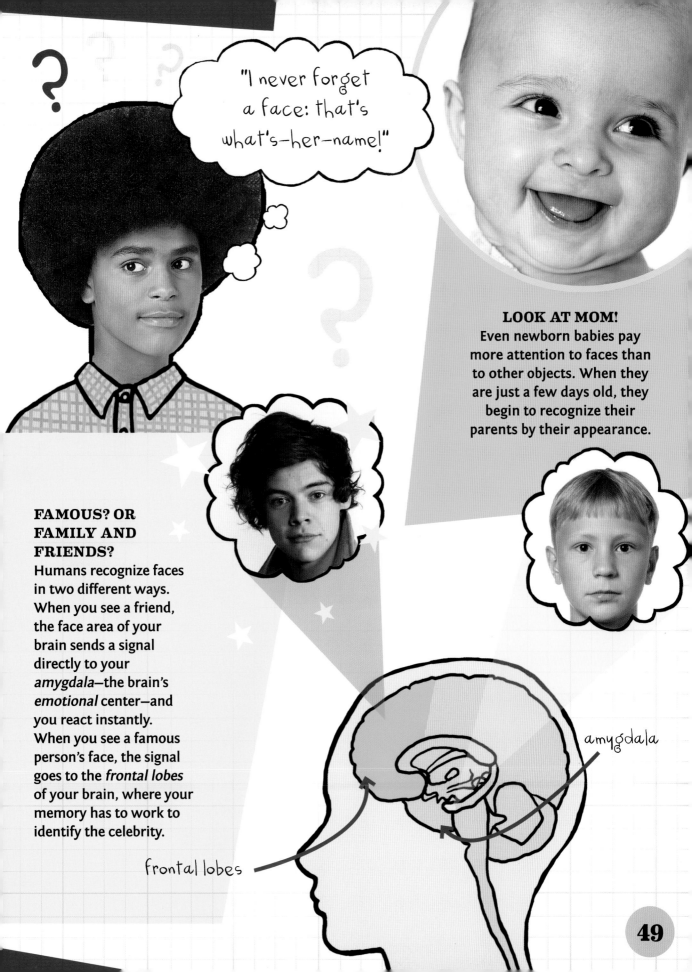

"I never forget a face: that's what's-her-name!"

LOOK AT MOM!
Even newborn babies pay more attention to faces than to other objects. When they are just a few days old, they begin to recognize their parents by their appearance.

FAMOUS? OR FAMILY AND FRIENDS?
Humans recognize faces in two different ways. When you see a friend, the face area of your brain sends a signal directly to your *amygdala*—the brain's *emotional* center—and you react instantly. When you see a famous person's face, the signal goes to the *frontal lobes* of your brain, where your memory has to work to identify the celebrity.

amygdala

frontal lobes

WHOSE FACE?

It's easy to prove how special face recognition is. See if you can recognize the upside-down faces of the celebrities printed below.

Nothing signals happiness more clearly than a big fat grin. We use different *muscles* to twist our faces into these expressive shapes.

Can you identify the Big Six expressions?

Anger, disgust, fear, happiness, sadness, and surprise.

1

2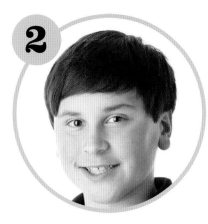

3

4

5

6

How many did you guess?

Check your answers on page 52

QUIZ ANSWERS

Whose Face?

Our special ability to recognize faces relies on us seeing them with the eyes at the top and the mouth at the bottom. Flipping faces fools our brains in a way that flipping pictures of other objects does not.

 1 Rihanna

 2 Beyonce

 3 Prince William

 4 Barack Obama

 5 Britney Spears

 6 Harry Styles

The Big Six Expressions

These "big six" expressions are fairly easy to recognize. Other faces do not have such obvious meanings. For example, we don't all use the same facial muscles when we feel guilt or regret.

 1 sadness

 2 happiness

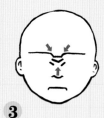 3 anger

 4 fear

 5 surprise

 6 disgust

SMILE!

Smiles don't always really mean happiness—but fakers are easy to spot. A genuine happy look exercises the whole face. People who are just pretending use only the *muscles* that yank up the corners of the mouth.

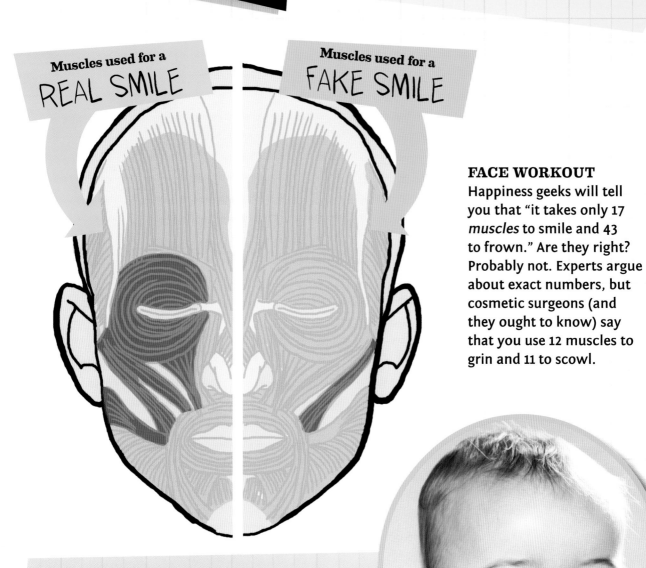

Muscles used for a
REAL SMILE

Muscles used for a
FAKE SMILE

FACE WORKOUT
Happiness geeks will tell you that "it takes only 17 *muscles* to smile and 43 to frown." Are they right? Probably not. Experts argue about exact numbers, but cosmetic surgeons (and they ought to know) say that you use 12 muscles to grin and 11 to scowl.

NO LEARNING REQUIRED!
Humans are born knowing how to look happy and sad—babies don't have to be taught to scowl or smile. How can we be sure? Because even people who are blind from birth smile when they are happy. They couldn't do that if they had to learn smiles by imitating their parents.

WHAT FACES TELL US

When we first meet people, we instantly judge what they are like by looking at their faces. In just one tenth of a second, we decide whether we like them, trust them, find them attractive, can rely on them—or fear them. What's more, these first impressions are so powerful that we are unlikely to change them. But are they accurate? Do faces lie?

MIRRORED FACE
(left side)

NORMAL FACE

MIRRORED FACE
(right side)

MATCHING LEFT AND RIGHT

Symmetrical faces have balanced opposite sides, as if one side was an exact mirror-image of the other. The more symmetrical a person's face, the more we judge them to be trustworthy and attractive. There is a biological reason for this. It is thought that facial symmetry may show that someone has a strong *immune system* and healthy *genes*. He or she will pass these genes on to his or her children, and so would make a good marriage partner.

RATE YOUR OWN SYMMETRY

To judge how *symmetrical* your own face is, hold a mirror over the centerline of a photograph. You might be surprised at how different your left and right sides are!

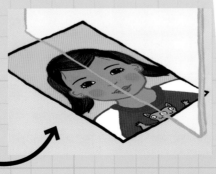

MASCULINE OR FEMININE?

Strongly male or female features result from the sex *hormones*— chemicals in our blood that make us men or women. We use these features to judge people we meet. Strongly feminine faces attract men because women with lots of the *estrogen* hormone have babies easily. For similar reasons, women may choose "mannish" men if they want to start a family. However, lots of the *testosterone* hormone can also make men into bullies.

Lots of the female hormone, *estrogen*, gives women small noses and chins, large eyes, and full lips.

Testosterone, the male hormone, makes men hairy and enlarges their jaws and eyebrows.

Average male face

Average female face

MORE ATTRACTIVE THAN AVERAGE?

The most attractive faces don't really exist! Scientists merged hundreds of different faces to create an "average" face that belonged to no real person. People who look at this invented face rated it as more attractive than other, real-life, faces.

THE FACE OF A VILLAIN

Victorian scientist Francis Galton was one of the first to create averaged faces—of criminals! He hoped to show that villains all had similar faces, so that police could easily spot them in a crowd. Although he failed, modern researchers have linked wide male faces to violent behavior.

HOW DO I REMEMBER THINGS?

You're given a puppy for your 5th birthday.

What do you remember about it?

Sensations

- Warmth
- Licking
- Smell
- Barking
- Weather
- Appearance

Sensory memory

Only holds a few items, and they vanish after **half a second or less.**

Paying attention
You concentrate on the brilliant surprise: the puppy and everything you like about it.

Forgotten

The useless stuff:
- The sounds you made when you tore open your presents.

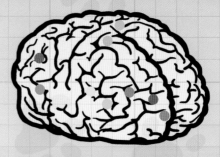

The memory is stored all over your brain in countless strengthened connections among your *neurons*.

- first sight of puppy in basket
- beige color of fur
- dad's shout when it bit him
- sound of bark
- wet feeling when it urinated on my foot
- softness of fur
- puppy smell
- name: Raymond
- breed: Labrador

Is this stuff neat enough to be remembered?

Yup! Puppy—cool!

dorsolateral prefrontal cortex

parietal lobe

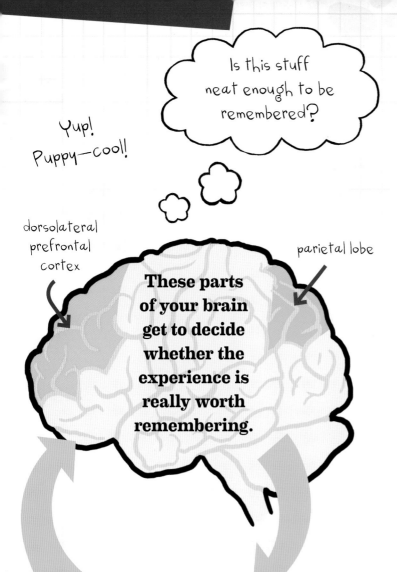

These parts of your brain get to decide whether the experience is really worth remembering.

Remembered

Short-term memory

Also stores only a little information, but lasts **half a minute.**

Processing
Much of it done by the *hippocampus*.

Long-term memory

Too big to measure! Lasts for ages—the "birthday puppy" memory will stay with you **all your life.**

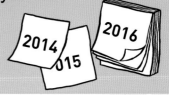

Forgotten

More useless stuff: what was for lunch; great Aunt Sally's dress; and the color of the wallpaper.

TEST YOUR MEMORY QUIZ ...

Finding out exactly how good your memory is takes the skill of a scientist. However, a few simple tests can give you a rough idea of how much you forget—and it's fun, too. Try these five tests, then read on...

QUIZ TIME!

1

FAMILIAR OBJECTS
Does the queen's head face left or right on a postage stamp?

?

2

SPINNING SHAPES IN YOUR MEMORY
Look at these pictures and try to decide whether the same object appears in each picture. Don't take longer than four seconds to decide on each one. Check your answers on page 60.

A

B

C

3

HOW MANY WORDS CAN YOU REMEMBER?

In the list below, read the words on the first line and try to remember them. Then—as before—cover the line with a piece of paper, and write the words down. Do the same with each line.

cabbage, Wednesday, yellow

France, soccer, Tuesday, armchair

water, Sunday, soft, strawberry, rabbit

healthy, November, cardboard, telephone, window, Japan

scissors, sunset, hungry, Africa, pirate, dreaming, television

pencil, Monday, table, astronaut, snake, temple, family, trousers

4

HOW MANY NUMBERS CAN YOU REMEMBER?

In the list below, read the first number and remember it. Then cover it with a piece of paper, and write the number down. Do the same with all the numbers in the list.

293

910

2,635

9,854

27,380

56,936

451,694

742,695

4,158,789

1,452,697

14,523,635

14,356,295

5

SPOT THE DIFFERENCE

Study this photograph carefully, then turn to the next page. (Don't cheat by turning back to this one to check!)

1 FAMILIAR OBJECTS

ANSWER: the queen faces to the left.
Got it wrong? Many of us do. We look at stamps every day, but pay surprisingly little attention to what's on them. Stamp collectors are better than average at this memory task, because what's on stamps matters more to them.

2 SPINNING SHAPES

ANSWER: B is the same as A. C is different from A.
This test shows how good your working memory is at turning objects. If you did well, you'll be good at moving house and can imagine how furniture will fit in your new rooms. On moving day, you will have no trouble packing awkwardly shaped objects so that they take up the least space. You may find sports easier, too. Generally, boys are a little better than girls at this test.

3 + 4 RECALLING WORDS AND NUMBERS

How many could you remember? Remembering more than about seven numbers or five words is pretty difficult. You probably spoke the lists out loud to try to remember them. It's partly the time this takes that limits your memory. Your working memory (see pages 56–57) can only hold a few seconds of information before it becomes full. If you scored badly, don't worry. Stress and tiredness reduce your ability to hold things in your head.

5 SPOT THE DIFFERENCE

Can you remember any differences between this picture and the one on the previous page? To see the answer below, turn the book upside down.

ANSWER: the empty parking space has changed.
This test reveals how well you remember a scene. If you didn't spot the difference, don't worry. Parking is unlikely to be a problem for you. But a driver will probably notice the change because he or she spends time hunting for parking spaces.

WHY DO I FORGET THINGS?

Almost everybody wishes they had a better memory. But when we complain that we forget things, what exactly do we mean? Do we have trouble remembering where we went on vacation five years ago? Or is it that we can't recall an important name?

Not remembering what we need to is a problem, but remembering everything would be worse. We experience so much, even in a single day, that the information would *overwhelm* us if we remembered all of it.

WHY DO SMELLS TRIGGER VIVID MEMORIES?

You step into a new building, sniff new paint, and suddenly memories of your first day at primary school come rushing back. Or the smell of warm chocolate reminds you of the first time you baked a cake.

Smells—and sometimes music—can bring back vivid, unexpected memories like no other sensations can.

But why?

CAKES AND MEMORY

The link between smell and memory is called the Proust effect, after French writer Marcel Proust. In his 1913 novel *In Search of Lost Time,* he describes how the smell of small, lemony madeleine cakes brought powerful, joyful memories of his childhood rushing back.

62

THE NOSE KNOWS!

We don't know the answer for sure, but memory scientists have tried hard to find out. By *scanning* the brains of people who are sniffing smells that are special to them, scientists can see which parts of the brain are especially active. The parts that glow brightest on brain scans are the *hippocampus* and the *amygdala*. These brain zones both work hard in processing memory and *emotion*. What's more, inside your skull, both are close to the *olfactory* bulbs, bean-sized smell-processing organs. No wonder there is such a strong link.

amygdala

hippocampus

olfactory bulbs

WHAT'S THAT TUNE?

Though not as powerful as smells, music can also bring back vivid memories. Scans show that familiar tunes and smells both activate similar areas in the brain—on the left side in most people, and the *hippocampus* in particular. Some experts think this means the two sensations work in similar ways.

WOULD I STILL BE ME IF I LOST MY MEMORY?

In the plots of countless cheesy movies, the hero gets a bump on the head, and promptly forgets who he or she is. In the final scene, of course, another bump brings his or her memory back—just in time to save the day.

But real life is never as neat as a Hollywood film. Though it's true that a blow to the head can cause temporary or permanent *amnesia* (memory loss), this can take dramatically different forms.

KEEPING THE BRAIN WORKING
People suffering from Alzheimer's disease lose their short-term memory, but at first may still recall their childhoods, for example. As the disease advances, more memories gradually slip away. Personality can be a little like the sum of someone's memories—as these fade, the person's character may change. He or she becomes less like the person their friends and family knew. Fortunately, drugs and exercising the brain and body can help to slow the disease's progress.

UNLOCKING MEMORY

Painting and reminiscence therapies can help Alzheimer's sufferers to access memories they thought they had lost. Music from the past also remains familiar and enjoyable long after real memories from the same time have gone.

DEGREES OF FORGETTING

Because amnesiacs usually keep some of their memories, their basic character does not change. This isn't true for people suffering from Alzheimer's disease, however. This disease slowly destroys brain tissue. Sufferers eventually forget who they are, and may not even recognize their own reflections.

WHEN MEMORY GOES WRONG

FORGETTING THE PAST— OR THE PRESENT

Many things can stop memory working. Accidents, *strokes*, brain *tumors* and even alcohol can do it. Backwards, or "retrograde," *amnesia* destroys memories of things that happened before the damage, like the empty compartments on the left. Forwards, or "anterograde," amnesia does the opposite. Memories following the damage weaken. Both types of memory may return with time.

Condition of Memory

	CHILDHOOD	RECENT PAST
Normal memory		
Backwards amnesia		
Forwards amnesia		
Early Alzheimer's disease		
Late Alzheimer's disease		

Remembered Event

1 YEAR AGO	1 MONTH AGO	YESTERDAY	1 MINUTE AGO	1 SECOND AGO

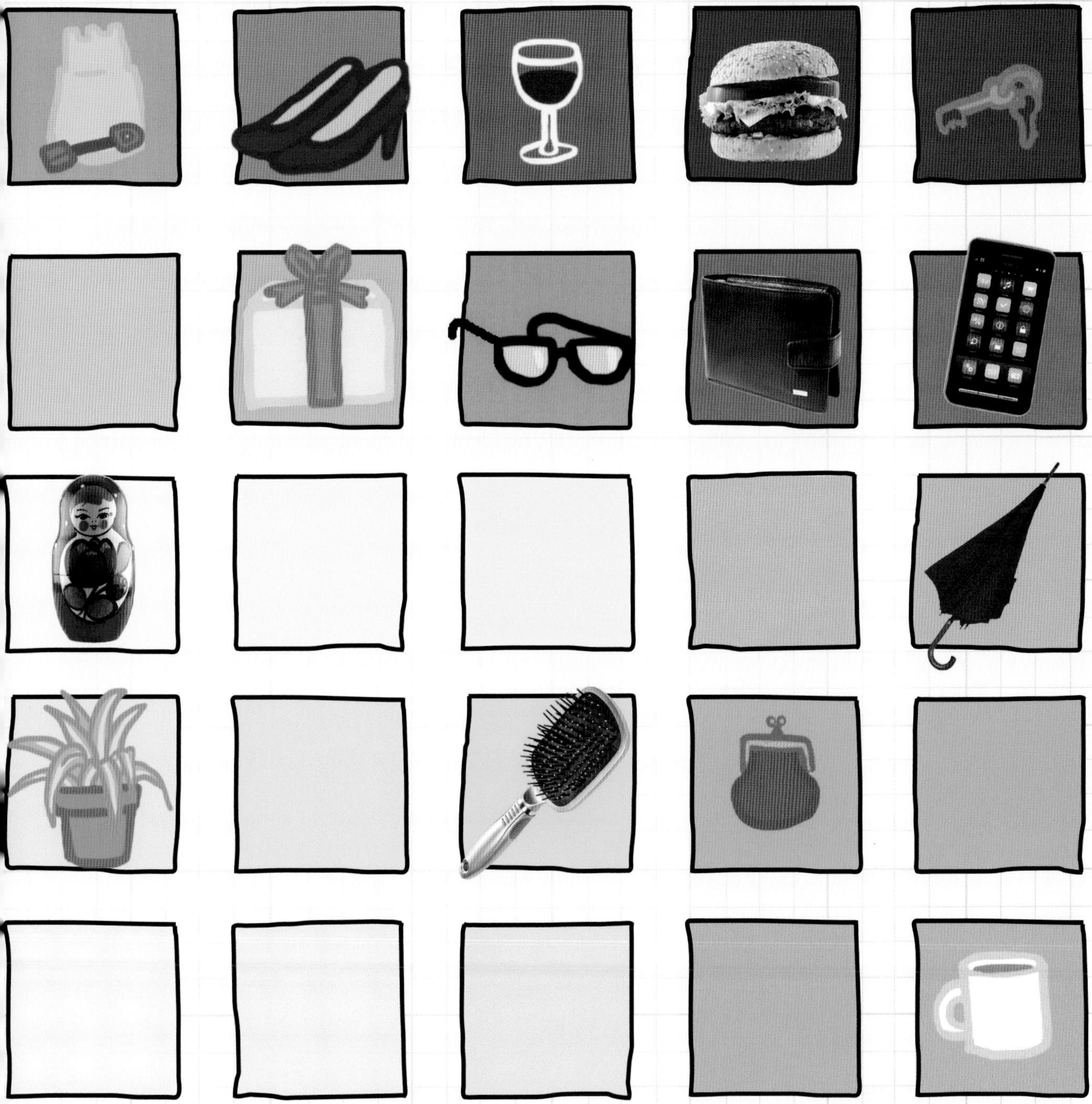

HOW CAN I IMPROVE MY MEMORY?

The best way to remember anything is to memorize it! This sounds like a dumb answer, but it's true. Recalling something you have learned earlier makes the memory stronger, especially if you do this over and over again. If you are studying for an exam, put away the textbooks and test yourself. Research proves this is the surest way to improve your ability to remember facts.

Learn French in one night!

Q CAN I LEARN A FOREIGN LANGUAGE BY LISTENING TO A CD WHILE I SLEEP?

A No.

Q HOW DO MEMORY EXPERTS REMEMBER SO MUCH STUFF?

A Performers can recall the order of several packs of cards—and even long lists shouted out by the audience. They do this by using the "method of places." They imagine a familiar room, or a journey they make regularly. Then they place each item they want to remember at different spots. To remember a shopping list, you could picture your walk to school. Melted cheese drips from the front doorknob. Carrots fill the front yard, and so on. The more outrageous the combination, the easier it is to remember.

Q WILL FISH OIL PILLS IMPROVE MY MEMORY?

A Fish oils contain lots of chemicals called omega-3 fatty acids. All humans need these chemicals for healthy growth, but your normal diet probably contains enough. Despite what advertisers tell you, fish oil tablets won't improve your memory. Nor will eating your goldfish.

Q WILL A "BRAIN BOOSTING" PROGRAM IMPROVE MY MEMORY?

A Computer- and console-based programs that claim to improve your memory, or "keep your brain fit and agile," are unlikely to make much difference to young people. However, some of these programs work for older people whose memory is getting worse.

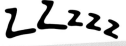

Q DOES IT MATTER WHEN I MEMORIZE STUFF?

A If you go to sleep immediately after studying something, you will remember it better. Timing helps in other ways, too. Memorization works best when you do it about one eighth of the way between learning and testing. So, if you first study a subject today, and you have a test in eight days time, tomorrow is the best day to memorize. But, sorry to say, if what you are studying is so dull that it actually puts you to sleep, you probably won't remember any of it!

CAN I TRUST MY SENSES?

Through *sense organs* such as your eyes and ears, you learn everything about the world around you. Because you use these senses all the time, you probably think you can rely on them. Think again! These simple experiments show just how much you take for granted. Try them out, then turn the page to find out more about the amazing world of sensation.

Experiment TIME!

Experiment 1

Fool your skin!
Get a friend to shut his or her eyes, then gently touch two toothpicks, held a tiny distance apart, against his or her fingertips. Does he or she feel one toothpick or two? Move the toothpicks further apart, and gently touch his or her skin again. Carry on until he or she feels two separate pricks, and write down the distance between them. Now do the same on his or her forearm. Your friend will find it much harder to feel two separate toothpicks on his or her arm when they are held close together.

Why does it work?
On the arm, pricks 2 in. (5 cm) apart still feel like a single prick because the *nerves* here are widely spaced. On our sensitive fingertips, the nerves are much closer together.

Experiment 2 👁

Fool your eyes!

Hold this book at arm's length. Close your left eye, and stare with your right eye at the green cross below. Now bring the book closer. At some point, the red dot will vanish (unless you swivel your eyeball to look directly at it).

Why does it work?

The *nerves* that detect light are spread out all over the back of your eye. But they are gathered together in a narrow bundle where the eye connects to the brain (see page 137). At the point on the eyeball where the nerves come together, the eye has a blind spot, which this test reveals.

Experiment 3 👅

Fool your tongue!

Take a raw potato and an apple. Peel both, then cut thin slices. Blindfold a friend and hold his or her nose so he or she cannot smell. Now feed him or her one slice of apple and one slice of potato, and challenge him or her to guess which is which. Bet they can't tell the difference!

Why does it work?

Your nose does much of the work in "tasting" food. Apples and potatoes have a similar texture—neither has a very sharp, salty, or sweet flavor for your tongue to detect. Smell is the only reliable way to tell them apart.

HOW AM I AWARE OF THE WORLD?

When we wake up each morning, sensations instantly bombard us. Light from the window dazzles us; the buzzing alarm clock deafens us; we smell coffee brewing; one arm aches from where we slept on it. Perhaps we feel too hot or cold, or have an urgent need to go to the bathroom! This wave of good and bad experiences comes from our *sense organs*: parts of our body that work as detectors, with the help of a rich supply of specialized *nerves*.

EYE
Your eye works like a camera. The clear lens at the front gathers light from a hole called the pupil. The resulting beam forms a sharp picture on the back of your eye. Cells there convert the brightness into a nerve signal that travels to your brain, giving you the sensation of seeing.

NOSE
Smells that waft into your nose dissolve in mucus, making a chemical soup. Hairlike cells covering a postage-stamp-size area inside the top of your nose detect these chemicals. The odor signals then travel to the brain along a special smell nerve.

SKIN AND ORGANS
Nerves in your skin give you a sense of touch, and much more. They sense heat and cold, pressure, vibration, tickle and pain. There are pain sensors in all your organs, too, though if illness or injury triggers them, you may feel pain in the skin nearby.

MUSCLES
Nerves in your muscles detect whether they are tense or limp. The signals they send to your brain allow you to judge where all your limbs are, and whether they are moving. Without this "body sense," called *proprioception*, even simple tasks like bending to pick something up would be impossible.

TONGUE
10,000 special cells in your mouth let you detect sweet, sour, salty, savory, and bitter flavors. These "taste buds" are mostly on the tongue. Nerves that cover the inside of each bud carry flavor signals to the brain.

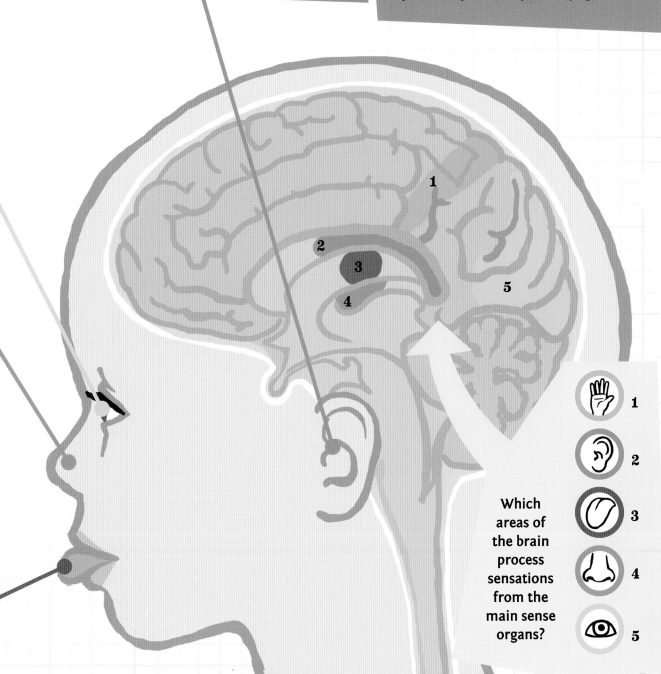

EAR

What we call sound is a rhythmic wave of pressure in the air. Sounds nearby make the stretched skin of your eardrum vibrate. Bones pressing against the drum increase the volume of these vibrations and carry them to a snail-shell-shaped tube. There, the vibrations make hairs inside wobble, tickling hearing nerves linked to the brain.

INNER EAR

Behind the hearing part of the ear are bony, fluid-filled channels that allow you to sense that you are moving. Your sense of "which way is up?" comes from this "inner ear," too. Tiny stones there use gravity to tug at a nerve-filled jelly layer to tell you when you're upright.

Which areas of the brain process sensations from the main sense organs?

1
2
3
4
5

HOW DO SENSATIONS GET TO MY BRAIN?

Your senses give you amazing powers. You can hear a pin fall to the floor in a quiet room, yet also enjoy rock music a million-million times louder. You can see in brilliant sunlight and also in dim starlight. Your eyes and ears don't perform these miracle feats on their own. They get masses of help from your brain. This processes the raw messages from your senses. Then, through some clever tricks, it turns them into what we call *perception*.

LIGHTNING FAST!

Taste, smell, sight, sound, and balance signals don't have far to go. But the sensation of pain you feel when a crab nips your right toe makes a longer journey. The "Youch!" feeling travels up your spine to the brain stem—the "switchboard" connecting the brain to your body. There, the nervous signals switch sides. So pain signals from your right toe go to the left side of your brain, and vice versa.

CONFUSING THREE SENSES

Next time you step off an amusement park ride, try to stand upright and think about what you are feeling. What we call dizziness is the sensation of three of your senses arguing. Tiny, fluid-filled tubes in your ears give you a sense of which way is up (see page 73), *nerves* in your *muscles* give you a sense of where your limbs are, and your eyes let you see the *horizon* (the line between sky and earth). Normally, these senses work together to keep you upright. But an amusement park ride moves so fast that the three senses send out very different messages. Then your poor brain gives up, and you throw up!

YOUCH!

SIGNAL TO SENSATION

A simple *nerve* impulse is just the beginning of a sensation. A whole lot goes on in your brain to turn the crude signals from your eyes and ears into that annoying toothpaste ad that's on in every commercial break! Different parts of your brain process the signals from each *sense organ*.

SEEING IS BELIEVING

When you look at a galloping horse, for example, different parts of your brain process the signals from your eyes in many different ways. Here's the information they extract:

MOVEMENT
The brain's ability to detect—and avoid—movement is vital if you don't want the sensation of hooves trampling your toes!

SHAPE
Your brain picks out the position and angle of lines in the scene, and processes them into a horse shape.

Experiment TIME!

SEEING THE INVISIBLE MOVING

Your brain is especially sensitive to any movement you see in the corner of your eye (perhaps because hungry beasts lurking just out of sight once threatened our *ancestors*). Test it like this: hold both hands close together at arm's length, at eye level, with the index fingers extended upwards. Keep staring straight ahead, and move your hands sideways until they just disappear on either side of your head. Now wiggle your index fingers. You'll see the movement, even if you can't clearly see the fingers.

PUTTING IT TOGETHER

Recognizing a horse from color, shape, depth, and movement requires even more processing, involving *knowledge* and memory.

DEPTH

Nervous signals from each eye are slightly different, enabling your brain to judge depth and distance.

COLOR

Three kinds of *cells* in your eyes each record red, green, or blue light. Their nervous signals combine in the brain to give you the sensation of color.

HOW DID I LEARN TO SPEAK?

Once we know how, speaking seems natural and easy. We cannot remember how we once struggled to say even a single word. It's only when, as adults, we try to learn a foreign language that we realize just how difficult speech can be.

AGE: 0

We hear speech as soon as we are born. (At least we hear it when we stop screaming.)

Average words: 0

AGE: 6 MONTHS

Long before they speak, babies understand what people say to them. Most children know the meaning of a few words before their first birthday.

Average words: 0

AGE: 12–18 MONTHS

Children "babble" when aged from six months to a year. Most manage a single word six months later.

Average words: 1

AGE: 18 MONTHS

Kids start to speak properly by linking words in pairs. However, they may not yet fully understand what they are saying.

Average words: 20

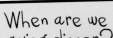

AGE: 2 YEARS

Language takes off at two, when children begin to make sensible sentences of three or four words.

Average words: 200

AGE: 4 YEARS

Two years later, most children have learned to put together quite long sentences, but often make errors.

Average words: 1,200

AGE: 10 YEARS

Before they reach their teens, children's language learning is almost complete, though they will continue to learn new words all their lives.

Average words: 16,000

AGE: 14 YEARS

Knowing how to speak in proper sentences does not mean that you have to do so.

Average words: 20,000

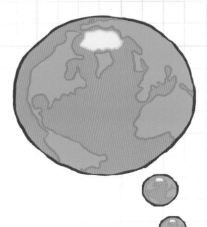

DON'T WAIT!

Why speak one language when you could speak two? It's possible to learn a second language at any time in your life. However, the younger you start, the easier it is and the better at it you will be.

HOW DO WORDS REACH MY LIPS?

3 A thick bundle of *nerve* fibers carries a message about the sounds to Broca's area. This region of the brain figures out how you need to move your *muscles* to make the correct sounds.

2 *Nerves* then carry the words to a region near your ear called Wernicke's area. Here, the brain matches the words to the sounds you make to speak them.

1 Speech begins in the temporal lobe. Here the brain takes the idea you want to talk about, and searches your memory for the words to describe it.

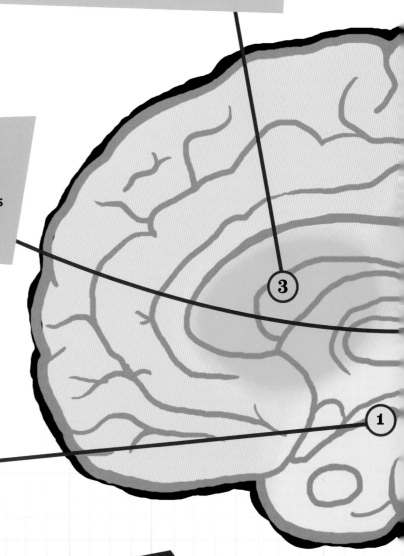

Lost for words? Blame your brain! Speaking is one of the most complex activities that humans can do. Once you have decided what you are going to say, *nerve* impulses ping through five separate regions of your brain to put words into your mouth.

4 Next in line is a part of the motor cortex that controls the parts of your body that you use to speak. This sends the nervous signals that activate the correct movements.

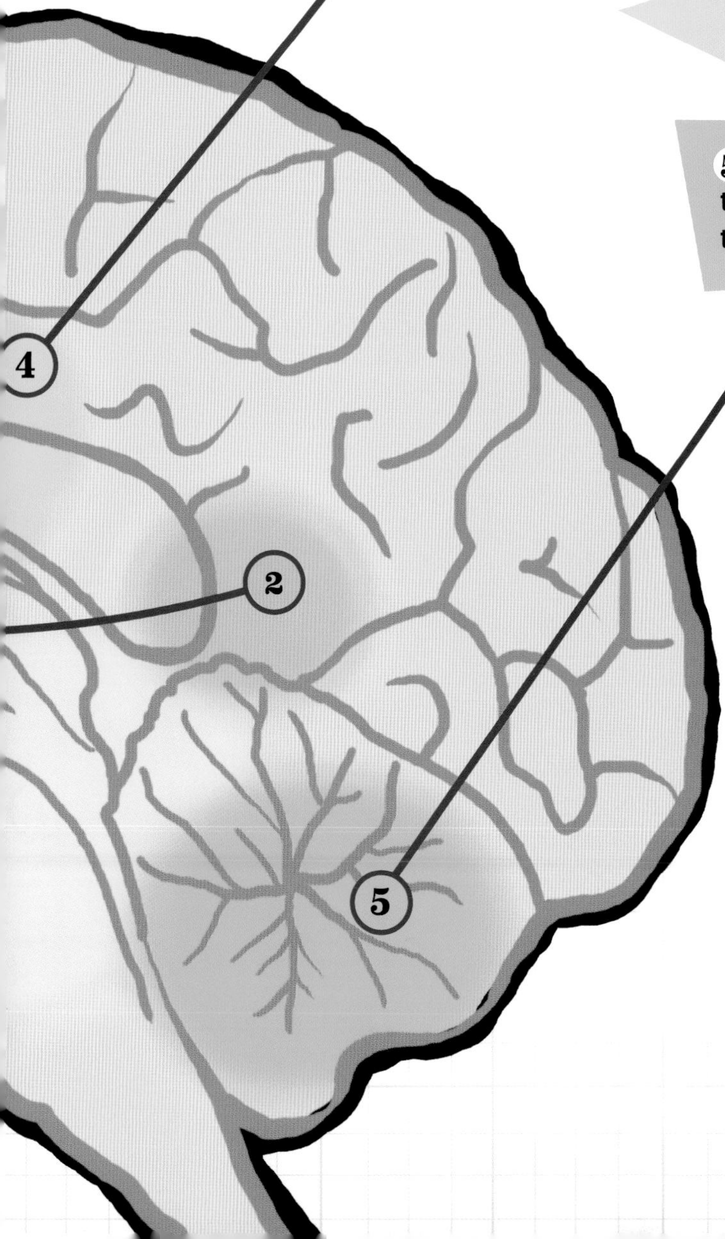

5 The *cerebellum* at the back of the brain fine-tunes the timing of the movements, and finally...

6 Your throat, tongue, and lips move to say the words you were thinking of a quarter of a second earlier.

4

2

5

Hello!

HOW DO I COMMUNICATE?

How long could you go without speaking? An hour? A day? Try it (and don't cheat by writing notes). Silence is more difficult than you might imagine, for speech is an easy way to tell others what we want or need. Talking quickly spreads ideas and *knowledge*, and it binds us together in our families and communities when we share our hopes, our dreams, and the stories that are important to us.

SAY IT WITH WAGS
Talking is not the only way to communicate, as any dog will tell you. Doggie language is all about facial expressions, wagging tails, and sniffing other dogs! But since *humans* learned to talk, at least 100,000 years ago, we have come to rely more on speech than on other ways of communicating. We haven't entirely stopped using gestures and expressions, though—see pages 51–52 and 84–87.

DOES TALKING MAKE US HUMAN?

Humans are specially equipped for talking. Vibrating skin folds in our throats—called vocal chords—make basic sounds, and our mouths and lips shape these sounds into words. Animals likewise communicate with sounds (and in other ways), but their "talking" is much simpler. Only with human speech is it possible to discuss whether aliens exist or Lady Gaga's stage outfits.

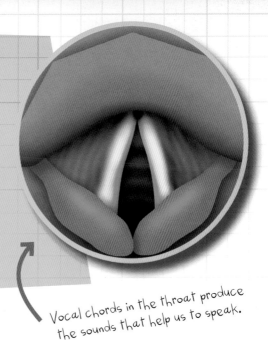

Vocal chords in the throat produce the sounds that help us to speak.

SAY IT IN WRITING

Writing words down made human communication even more powerful. Until sound recording and telephones, speech didn't travel far, and lasted only as long as an echo. Writing traveled further and lasted longer—and even today, e-mails, texts, and letters break barriers of time and distance.

A WORLD IN A WORD

Language has helped enable our *species, homo sapiens*, to become the most successful creatures on the planet. Speech allowed early humans to help each other and work together, and to pass on what they learned to their children.

83

CAN I SPEAK WITHOUT WORDS?

We don't just use our mouths to talk. Our faces and bodies join in the conversation, too, whether we like it or not.

We can even talk without words, using expressions, *gestures* and "body language."

"Honest, man!"

Some wordless gestures just make what we are trying to say stronger. This boy is saying,

"Look, I am being straight with you. You can trust me."

His outstretched arms show that he is not hiding anything in his hands.

DIRTY LOOKS NEED NO TRANSLATION

People from every race and continent recognize the same basic emotional faces. However, they may read them slightly differently. Compared to Europeans and Americans, people from East Asia look more at the eyes. Overlooking the rest of the face means that they may confuse fear with surprise and disgust with anger (see pages 51–52).

WHEN SPEECH STOPS WORKING

Because you use so many areas of your brain to speak, damage to just one of them can make talking more difficult. Known as aphasia, the disability may be slight, or it can stop speech altogether. Aphasia can have peculiar effects, too. Some sufferers are able to sing, but not to speak. Many autistic children suffer from aphasia.

BODY LANGUAGE AROUND THE WORLD

That's not what I meant at all!

Hand movements can mean different things in different parts of the world, so you need to be very careful how you use them when you are far from home. For example, in the U.K. and U.S., making a ring out of your thumb and index finger means "Everything's OK" or "Great!." But in Greece, the same gesture is one of the worst insults you can give.

TAPPING THE NOSE

Can mean:

"We're both in this together, you and I."

"Watch out!"   "You are too nosy!"

"I'm on the alert."   "He's smart!"

"I am threatening you."

TOUCHING THE EAR

Can mean:

"He's not a real man."

"Watch out!"   "Good!"

"He tries to get money out of people."

"Let's hope we are lucky."

"He is a sneak."

"I don't believe you."

SCREWING THE CHEEK

Can mean:

Good!"

"He's not a real man."

"You are crazy!"

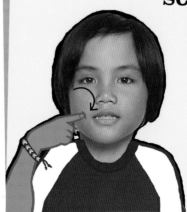

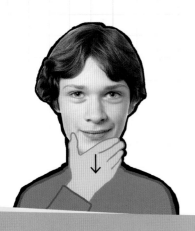

FINGERS CROSSED

Can mean:

"Let's hope we are lucky."

"Stay out of trouble."

"OK, good!"

"You are not my friend any more."

"We're friends."   "I promise."

STROKING THE CHEEK

Can mean:

"He's sick and thin."

"She's attractive!"

"I'm thinking about it."

"I'm winning."   "I'm sad."

"I'm threatening you."

"You are crafty."

FLICKING THE CHIN

Can mean:

"I'm not interested."

"No!"

"I don't believe you."

FINGER RING

Can mean:

"OK, great!"

"You're a zero, worth nothing."

"I'm threatening you."

TOSSING BACK THE HEAD

Can mean:

"No."   "Hi!"   "Come here!"

"Are you looking for trouble?"

"Come and get it!"

"I'm better than you."

"Can you explain that?"

HOW CAN I CONTROL MY EMOTIONS?

You're terrified! You freeze, your skin prickles, your palms sweat, your guts feel knotted, your heart races, and you're ready to run. An emotional response like this is a reminder of the animal that lurks inside all of us. We need *emotions* such as fear and happiness to thrive and to protect us from serious harm. Sometimes, though, emotions just seem to cause us trouble.

Dear Richard
I blush easily, and get teased for it. What should I do?

Emotions happen in your brain, but they affect your body. *Blushing* is a typical sign of embarrassment caused by the release of a hormone called *adrenaline*. The actual feeling of embarrassment is controlled by a thumb-sized region at the front of the brain. Fortunately, most of us grow out of excessive blushing. Give it time.

Dear Richard

My emotions often overtake me, and I say things I regret later. How can I control my feelings?

You will learn to control your emotions as you grow up. *Emotions* come from part of your brain called the *limbic system*. As well as strongly affecting your mood, they allow you to react without really thinking about threats, delights, affection, and the unexpected. They may be inconvenient, but without them you could not take split-second decisions—or fall in love.

Dear Richard
My friend keeps daring me to do crazy things. They sound like fun when he describes them, but something doesn't seem quite right. What do you advise?

Your friend's words have been reassuring, but his expressions and *gestures* may have alerted you to his own silent doubts. Even if your logical brain says "Yes!," your emotional response is to say "No." People call this a *gut reaction* or *intuition*. Sometimes following your intuition —or letting your heart rule your head—can help you to avoid trouble.

Dear Richard
My dad wants me to eat fish, but just the smell of it makes me gag! What can I do?

URRRGH!

Disgust protected our ancestors from eating dangerous foods. Today, most foods we buy are safe, but some of us still react emotionally to certain dishes. Within your brain—and probably on the right side—it's the part called the insula that makes you feel sick when you smell fish. "Meaty" fish like tuna may be easier to eat.

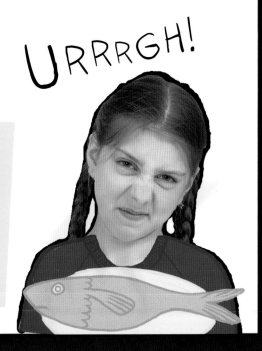

HOW CAN I BE FEARLESS?

Comic-book heroes fear nothing. Protected by their legendary super-powers, they swoop down to save the girl, the city, or the world. Wouldn't it be great to be just as brave? Maybe not. Fleeing from danger is often the most sensible and safe thing to do.

Are you SCARED?

What frightens you? The dark? Snakes? Spiders? The unknown? Scary things like these trigger familiar feelings. Our first response is usually to keep absolutely still. Then we run away, as fast as we can.

Both these reactions helped our *ancestors* to stay safe. Because dangerous animals see movement much more clearly than they see shape, ancient people survived attack from hungry tigers by keeping perfectly still. Then, upon seeing their chance, they made a mad dash to put some serious distance between them and some very sharp teeth!

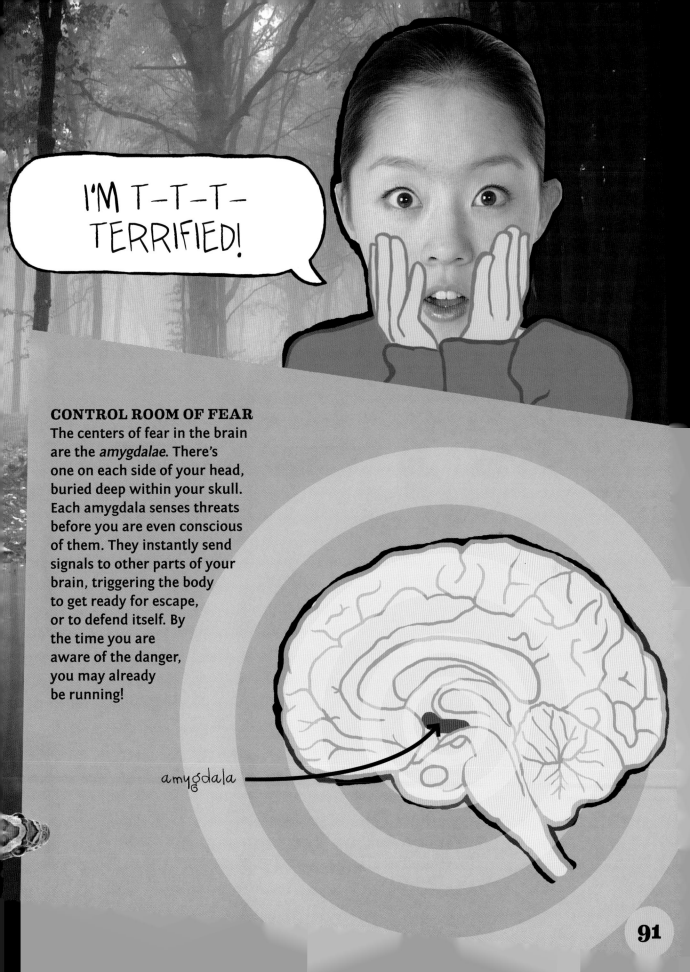

I'M T–T–T– TERRIFIED!

CONTROL ROOM OF FEAR

The centers of fear in the brain are the *amygdalae*. There's one on each side of your head, buried deep within your skull. Each amygdala senses threats before you are even conscious of them. They instantly send signals to other parts of your brain, triggering the body to get ready for escape, or to defend itself. By the time you are aware of the danger, you may already be running!

amygdala

HOW DOES FEAR AFFECT THE BODY?

When you are scared, signals from your *amygdalae* flood your body with *hormones* (chemicals in your blood) to prepare you for action.

Here are some of the effects...

ORGAN

Heart	Main Arteries	Lungs

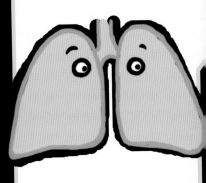

EFFECT

Speeds up	Get wider	Breathe faster

PURPOSE

Makes blood surge around the body, ready to supply the muscles for fast vigorous action	Distributes blood to arms and legs, and to the brain, for figuring out the best response	Draws into the body the extra oxygen needed for maximum effort

WAAAHHH!

Eyes

Pupils get bigger

Lose vision around the edges

Improves vision to help spot threats in dim light

Helps you concentrate on the danger staring you in the face

Liver

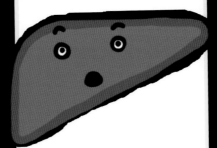

Releases sugars into the blood

Provides muscles with the fuel they need for action

Spleen

Makes extra *red blood cells*

These cause blood to clot, stopping bleeding in case you are injured

WHAT AM I AFRAID OF?

Keeping away from a snarling dog may save you from a bite. But if ALL dogs frighten you, then you have a *phobia*. Phobias are fears of things that are usually harmless. Most people with phobias cope with them by avoiding everything that frightens them. However, this can greatly limit their lives.

WHAT CAUSES PHOBIAS?

Bad experiences can cause phobias. For example, a bite from a savage dog may give you a life-long fear of dogs (we call this cynophobia).

ARE PHOBIAS COMMON?

Fear is an important emotion. It triggers reactions in your body that allow you to fight danger or run away quickly. *Phobias* are extreme fears of places, situations, animals or objects.

Did you know that about one person in every eight in the U.K. has a phobia?

Or that women are twice as likely to have a phobia as men?

Some experts think that parents can pass on phobias to their children in their genes. For example, identical *twins* often share the same phobia even when they are brought up separately. Do several people in your family share a phobia?

FAMOUS people with phobias

DAVID BECKHAM has a fear of disorder and untidiness. This is called **ataxophobia**.

THE MOST COMMON PHOBIAS ARE:

- a fear of SPIDERS
- a fear of THUNDER
- a fear of OUTSIDE
- a fear of SNAKES
- a fear of HEIGHTS

LIAM PAYNE from One Direction has **koutaliaphobia**, which is a fear of spoons.

SOME OF THE WEIRDEST PHOBIAS ARE:

- a fear of LONG WORDS
- a fear of SWALLOWING
- a fear of BEARDS
- a fear of MIRRORS
- a fear of BUTTONS

ORLANDO BLOOM is afraid of pigs— otherwise known as **swinophobia**.

IS THERE A CURE?
The good news is that three-quarters of people who suffer from serious phobias can overcome them. Often, just gradually facing up to the cause of the phobia can make the fear go away.

95

HOW CAN I BE HAPPIER?

Everybody agrees that happiness is a good thing, but describing exactly what it is isn't easy. It's not just the opposite of sadness.

It lasts longer than pure pleasure—though it may not be so intense. And, surprisingly, it doesn't have much to do with getting rich. So if you want to be happier, be very careful what you wish for!

GIMME MONEY!

Poverty makes everybody miserable, but—in spite of what you would expect—getting rich won't make you happy. Most people have far more money and stuff than their grandparents, but they are no happier.

PLEASURE YOU CAN MEASURE

Pleasant things tickle a special part of your brain. Low down, and near the back, this pleasure center releases a kind of "happy chemical" called dopamine. It's when *dopamine* reaches the thinking, *frontal lobes* of your brain that you realize you are having fun. Dopamine levels allow brain scientists to measure pleasure.

PLAYER OR ADDICT?

Gambling, drugs, and playing video games all release *dopamine*. A craving for the feelings of pleasure this chemical brings can lead to a dangerous addiction to any of these activities.

Don't worry

GET HAPPY!

There are some practical ways to make yourself happy. OK, these ideas sound silly, but experiments have proved that they work. Here's what experts suggest:

GRaTeFUL DiaRy

- Keep a diary of things for which you are grateful.

- Regularly do kind and unselfish things, such as volunteering or helping others.

- Write down at bedtime three things that went well that day.

- Identify your best qualities, and work out new ways to make use of them.

FIVE THINGS THAT MAKE YOU HAPPY

Scientists researching happiness suggest that it comes from **FIVE** main things:

1 PLEASANT THINGS

Enjoyable experiences such as eating food you like, or pampering yourself in a hot bath.

yum!

2 ACHIEVING

This means setting yourself goals, and making sure that you reach them.

1ST PLACE WINNER

3 CHALLENGING, ENJOYABLE ACTIVITY

Doing stuff that you like and that stretches your abilities.

4 RELATIONSHIPS

Friends and family really do make you happy.

5 BELONGING

Don't just focus on "ME." Your life will have more meaning if you work with others toward a goal you all share.

WHAT'S THE POINT OF ANGER?

When *humans* lived in caves and fought each other for the last mammoth steak on the grill, anger was a valuable emotion. It allowed us to react quickly when others threatened us, or took what was ours.

Today, anger is rarely as useful. It can even spoil our lives and make us ill.

Hisssss

ANIMAL ANGER

Look at an angry cat. Its hair stands on end, making it look huge and scary. Its teeth are bared, its legs go stiff, and it spits. Human anger isn't always so spectacular, but it's still a very physical *emotion*. It makes us twist our faces and bodies into shapes that threaten and frighten others.

WHERE DOES
ANGER
COME FROM?

Brain scans show that when people are angry, there's an area of the brain just behind the eyes that becomes very active. Its name? The lateral orbitofrontal cortex. (Don't you wish you hadn't asked?)

lateral orbitofrontal cortex

ANGER GENE
Yes, there are *genes* linked to anger, too. For example, people who get angry easily may have a different version of a gene that affects the "happy" chemical, *dopamine* (see page 96). So if your mom or dad are often angry, you're more likely to be, too.

SHOULD YOU TRY TO CONTROL ANGER?

People who get really angry, really easily often run into difficulty. Their reaction to everything is to fight—with fists, or just harsh words.

As well as leading to social problems, anger pours two hormones—*adrenaline* and *cortisol*—into the blood. If you are constantly angry, your blood pressure will rise, and you will get sick more easily.

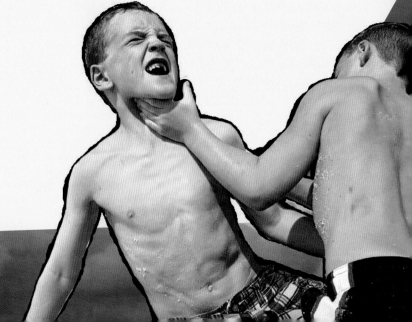

WHEN ANGER BECOMES A PROBLEM
Everybody gets angry from time to time. It's a natural emotion. Unless you suffer extreme or frequent anger, it's probably not good to hide it. Better to show that you are angry, but avoid a real fight.

COPING WITH ANGER?

It's hard to control yourself when someone or something makes you angry, but if you can remember to,

THINK RAGE...

Is this **REALLY** important? 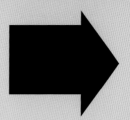 Don't get mad about small things.

Is my reaction **APPROPRIATE?**  Anger is not always the best way to react.

Will anger have a **GOOD** effect?  Don't get angry about things you can't change and be wary of doing something you will regret.

Will I be better off at the **END?**  Make sure that any action you take is worthwhile.

WHAT DOES IT MEAN TO BE A BOY OR A GIRL?

When you first meet someone, what's the first thing you notice?

It's not their height, the sound of their voices, or the color of their hair. It's their gender. This vital difference between male and female is decided at the very moment that life itself begins.

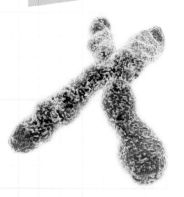

Q HOW WAS MY GENDER DECIDED?

A Whether you are born a boy or a girl is like flipping a coin: there is no simple way of controlling or predicting the result. Like so much about us, gender is decided by *genes*. Two *chromosomes* (see page 18) affect it. Because of their shape, they are called X and Y chromosomes. Girls have two X chromosomes; boys have one of each.

Q YES, BUT HOW DO I GET MY GENDER CHROMOSOMES?

A We all start out female! A woman's *eggs*—her gender *cells*—contain only X *chromosomes*. It's *sperm* (the male gender cell) that decides whether the egg will become a boy or a girl. Half of all sperm carry a Y chromosome; the other half, an X. When a man and a woman try to have a baby, the man releases millions of sperm cells. However, only one can merge with the egg that the woman produces each month. If the sperm carries a Y chromosome, the egg will develop into a baby boy. If it carries an X chromosome, a girl is created.

Q BUT TINY BABIES LOOK PRETTY SIMILAR!

A You can spot the difference on even the smallest babies if you look between their legs! But even this difference only begins to appear after about 11 weeks of development inside the mother. Before that, male and female fetuses (unborn children) are hard to tell apart.

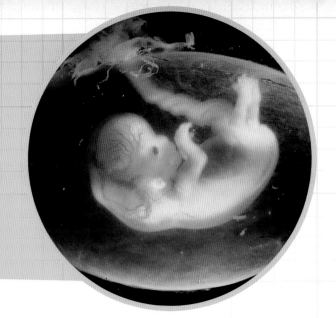

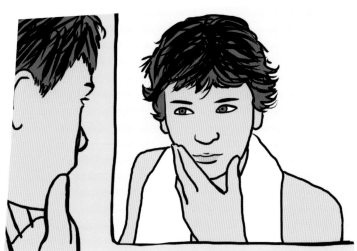

Q SO WHAT MAKES THE GENDER DIFFERENCES MORE OBVIOUS?

A Before birth, genes do most of the work in making a fetus male or female. Gradually, though, hormones (the body's signaling chemicals) become more important. Their power surges at puberty in the early teenage years. That's when gender hormones trigger the body changes that make adults obviously men or women.

Q WHY DO SOME PARENTS HAVE CHILDREN ALL OF THE SAME GENDER?

A Most men produce a roughly equal mix of X and Y *sperm*. However, a gene controls the exact ratio. In a few unusual families, the father may produce far more of one sort of sperm—in which case, the parents might have 3, 4, or even 5 boys or girls in a row.

DO I THINK AND REACT DIFFERENTLY FROM THE OPPOSITE GENDER?

Men and women are different—that's obvious. But do the differences go beyond the shapes of our bodies, and, if so, why?

BUSY BRAINS
Medical *scanners* measure blood flow to show which parts of our brains are busiest (see page 40). A woman looking at emotional pictures has a busy left-side brain. The effect on a man's brain is smaller.

TRUE or FALSE?

BOYS PREFER TOY CARS TO DOLLS
Boys and girls really do choose different toys. It's a biological difference—even male monkeys play more with toy cars.

WOMEN CAN'T READ MAPS
Not true! Despite this old joke, scientists have found there is little difference in navigation skills between the two genders.

MY BRAIN'S BIGGER!
Men tend to have bigger brains than women, in line with their bigger bodies—but male brains contain no more of the vital gray stuff where all the thinking goes on.

WOMEN CRY MORE

Yes: four times as much. The different shape of their tear ducts may be a clue—plus they make more of the *hormone* that triggers crying.

WOMEN ARE MORE EMOTIONAL

Actually, they're not! Men are simply taught to hide what they are feeling, but the emotions are still there.

MEN ARE FIGHTERS

Not by much. Women can be almost as aggressive, but usually learn not to show it.

WOMEN GET DEPRESSED MORE

True, but why?
We've yet to find the answer.

MATH, LEADERSHIP, AND TALKING

Are these especially male or female skills? Assumptions aside, tests show no real difference between the genders.

WHY ARE BOYS AND GIRLS DIFFERENT?

BOY

There are three possible reasons why men and women may think and act differently:

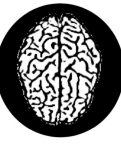

BIOLOGY

Physical differences in the brain. Take a knife and fork to male and female brains and you can see a few differences. Brain scans show increased activity in different areas, too.

TRAINING

This alters how we behave, encouraging boys to "act like a man" and girls to be "ladylike." But it can't explain everything.

HORMONES

The signaling chemicals that flow through our blood are quite different between men and women. They help explain why we feel, say, and do what we do.

GENES AND LEARNING

So are we really born with a male or a female brain? Probably not. In general, men and women think in very similar ways, though there are some small differences. Some of these differences are caused by *genes*, but many are not. As we grow up, we learn how other people expect us to behave, and this affects our own "maleness" or "femaleness."

GIRL

HOW MALE OR FEMALE IS MY BRAIN?

How we behave, what we find easy or difficult, how we react to other people—our gender affects all these things, and many more. Take this test to see whether your brain is more MALE or FEMALE.

QUIZ TIME!

1 YOU'RE IN A GROUP HAVING A LAUGH. WHAT DO YOU CONTRIBUTE?

1. I can't tell jokes so I just listen and laugh along.
2. I know all the best jokes, so I have my friends in stitches.

2 YOU LOSE YOUR WAY ON A JOURNEY. WHAT DO YOU DO?

1. I stop and ask someone the way.
2. I look at the map AGAIN and try to work out where I went wrong.

3 YOUR BEST FRIEND'S GRANNY DIES, AND HE OR SHE IS REALLY UPSET ABOUT IT. HOW DO YOU RESPOND?

1. I call him or her and sympathize.
2. I call him or her and remind him or her that everyone has two grannys, and ask if the other one is still alive.
3. I think of a different reason for meeting, then just wait for him or her to talk about it.
4. I just leave him or her be—he or she needs time alone to get over it.

4 WHAT MAKES YOU THINK TO CALL YOUR BEST FRIEND?

1. I call him or her anytime, just to chat.
2. I only call when there's something specific I want to talk about.

5

YOU'RE HELPING YOUR MOM CHOP CHILIES AND THE KNIFE CUTS YOUR HAND. IT'S NOT SERIOUS, BUT IT REALLY HURTS. WHAT DO YOU DO?

1. I yell until someone comes to put a bandage on it.
2. I run it under the tap and pretend it doesn't hurt.
3. I let the tears flow—they help me forget the pain.
4. I wouldn't be helping to cook dinner in the first place.

6

YOU DO A PUZZLE WITH LOTS OF ODD-SHAPED PARTS PACKED TIGHT IN A BOX. HOW EASY IS IT TO REPACK IT?

1. It's difficult.
2. It's easy!

7

YOU'RE CHOOSING A NEW STEREO. HOW DO YOU DECIDE?

1. I ask my friends for their advice.
2. I pick the loudest one.
3. I go to the store and listen to some music on it.
4. I find a good website and read up on the tech specs.

8

A FRIEND GETS SOME NEW JEANS THAT REALLY DON'T SUIT HIM OR HER. WHAT DO YOU DO?

1. I say I like them, but then when he or she wears something different I'm a lot more enthusiastic.
2. I tell him or her the truth. It hurts at first, but at least he or she won't embarass him- or herself.

SCORING...

For each ODD **numbered answer,** ADD 1 **to your score**

For each EVEN **numbered answer,** SUBTRACT 1 **from your score**

How did you do?
(And why?)

Negative **scores suggest your brain is** male.
Positive **scores suggest your brain is** female.

The larger **the number in either direction, the** stronger **your male or female reactions and abilities.**

MEN tend to be slightly better at imagining shapes in space, and are more inclined to organize and decide things by facts and information. They typically hide their feelings, and like to dominate in groups.

WOMEN, on the other hand, are better at reading and adapting to others' moods and emotions, and are more likely to consider other people's opinions.

WHERE DID MY ANCESTORS COME FROM?

We are all apes! At least our *ancestors* were. In the distant past, apelike near-*humans* left their African forest homes for the plains. They gradually lost their body hair, learned to walk upright, to use tools, and to speak. They became what scientists call *homo sapiens*— the modern human *species* to which everyone alive today belongs.

ALL MIXED UP!

Most of us have very mixed-up origins. Though skin color makes each *race* look different, studying our *DNA* shows that we each contain a wide-ranging mix of genes. Even the most blue-eyed, blond-haired European, for example, has African *genes*. Island-dwelling people are the exception. Their *ancestors* always married people from the island, so they share less of their DNA with the rest of us.

WHAT WE ALL SHARE

Genetic scientists have unraveled and compared the *DNA* (see page 12) of many different people to discover how we gradually changed—or "*evolved*"—into modern *humans*. This research has also shown how amazingly similar we all are. If you stretched to a mile (1.6 km) DNA strands from any two humans, just 10 feet (3 m) actually affects how we grow and develop—and only two millimeters of that would be different for each person.

AM I REALLY JUST A NAKED CHIMP?

A chimpanzee is our nearest animal cousin. Out of every 20 parts of our *DNA*, chimps share 19. Don't rush to marry a chimp, though—we also share half of our DNA with the banana he's eating, and even more with the slug eating the skin!

THE REAL EVE?

Though all children have a mix of both parents' *genes*, mothers always pass on a special unchanged part of their *DNA* to their daughters. This "mitochondrial DNA," or mtDNA, allows us to follow our *species* back to the very first woman. Every *human* alive today is one of her *descendants*. Nicknamed "Mitochondrial Eve" after the Bible's first woman, she lived 200,000 years ago in what is now Tanzania, East Africa.

HOW DID I GET HERE?

By studying *DNA* recovered from long-buried *human* bones, scientists can trace the route our ancient *ancestors* took as they spread out across the world.

3 EUROPE

2

1

AFRICA

The Route

From **Africa**, humans moved first to the **Middle East**. From there, they spread to **Europe** and **Asia** before crossing the Pacific Ocean to **Australia** and **America**.

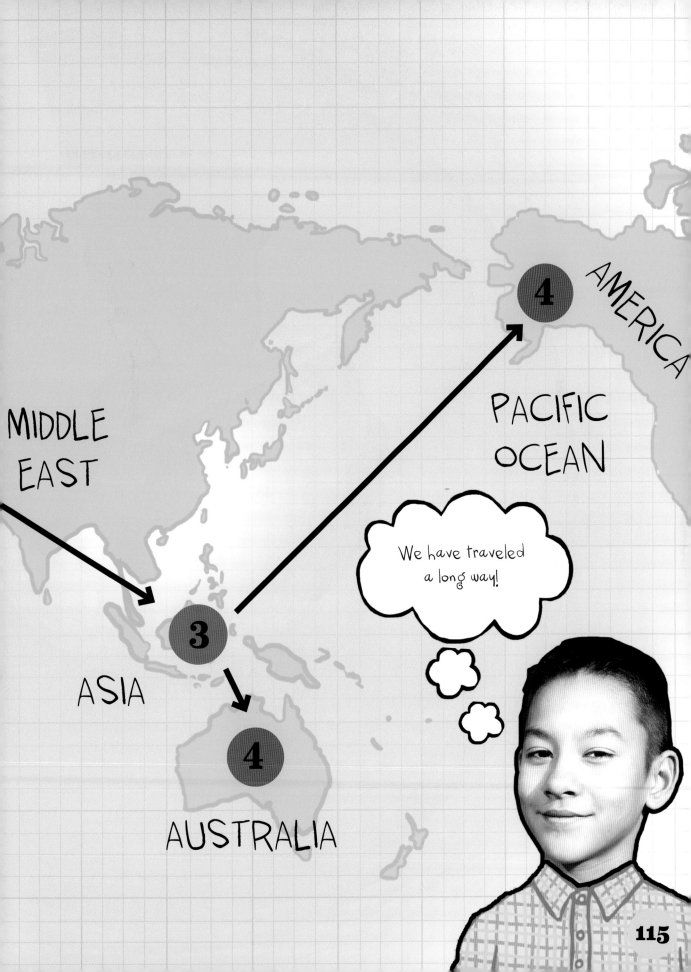

WHAT DO I KNOW ABOUT MY ANCESTORS?

Crumbling photo albums, spools of home movie film, and VHS cassettes gather dust in everybody's attics and closets. They seem like so much junk—until you want to find out more about your family's past.

Experiment TIME!

TREASURE IN THE ATTIC

Nothing brings genes and inheritance to life better than your own family. To see just how much you owe to your ancestors, dust off those albums, tapes, and films, and look at the pictures. Can you see yourself in any of the faces? The "family resemblance" is a visible sign of the invisible genes you share with your ancestors.

- Look especially at your parents and grandparents when they were your age.
- If you don't see yourself in a whole face, try covering everything except the eyes or the mouth.

TAKING IT FURTHER

If you want to learn more about where you came from and who you are related to, search the web for "family history." You will find links to public records and many other resources that will help you to find your *ancestors*.

A royal family tree from the 14th century

It has always been important for royalty to know exactly who those in line for the throne are descended from. You may not be destined for monarchy, but why not turn the page and follow the instructions for filling in your own family tree.

CLIMBING THE TREE

If you don't know your first cousin once removed from your grandnephew, see if one of your relations has drawn a family tree. In the chart below, each line of people is from the same *generation* (the same number of steps down from an *ancestor*).

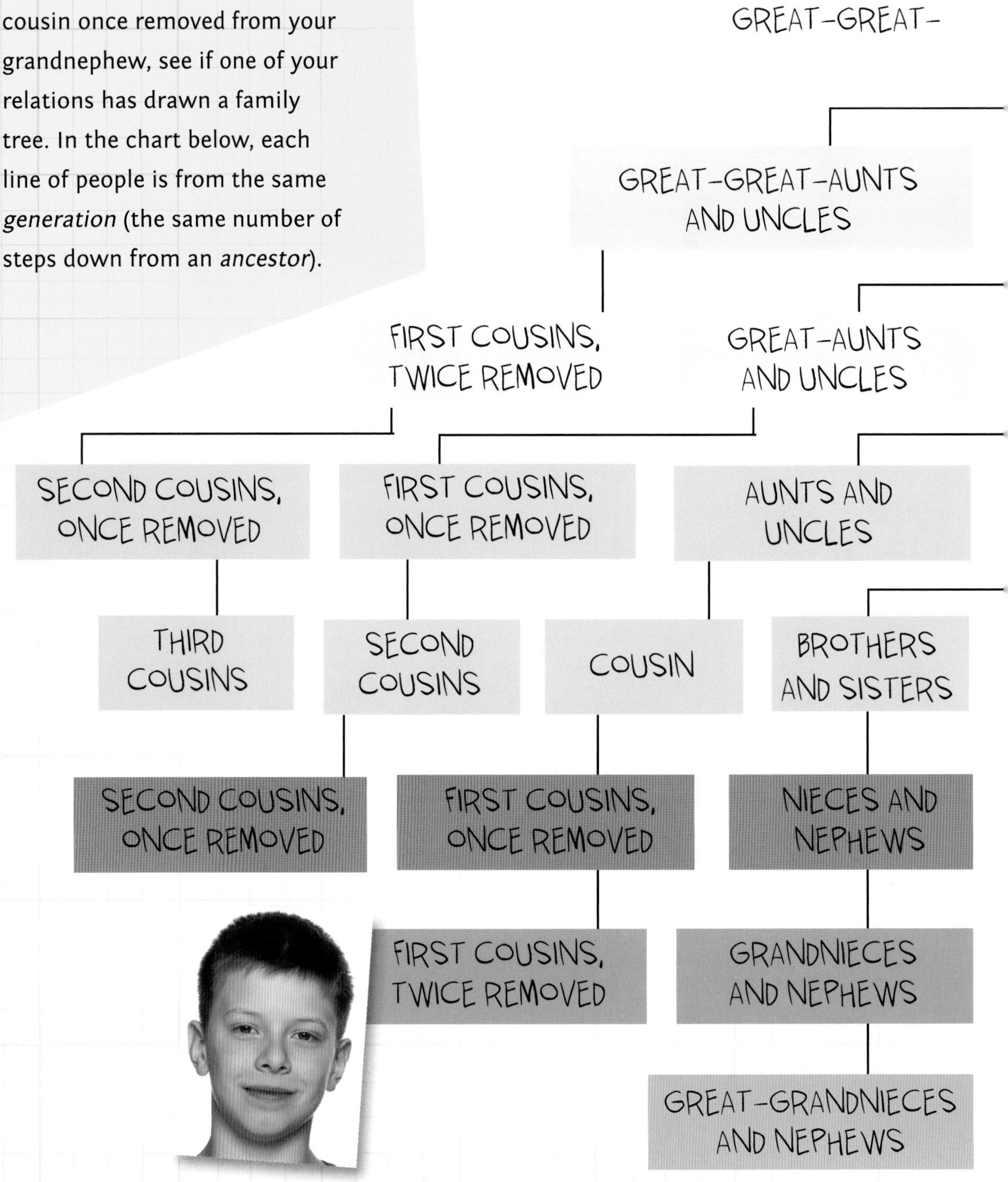

GREAT-GREAT-

GREAT-GREAT-AUNTS AND UNCLES

FIRST COUSINS, TWICE REMOVED

GREAT-AUNTS AND UNCLES

SECOND COUSINS, ONCE REMOVED

FIRST COUSINS, ONCE REMOVED

AUNTS AND UNCLES

THIRD COUSINS

SECOND COUSINS

COUSIN

BROTHERS AND SISTERS

SECOND COUSINS, ONCE REMOVED

FIRST COUSINS, ONCE REMOVED

NIECES AND NEPHEWS

FIRST COUSINS, TWICE REMOVED

GRANDNIECES AND NEPHEWS

GREAT-GRANDNIECES AND NEPHEWS

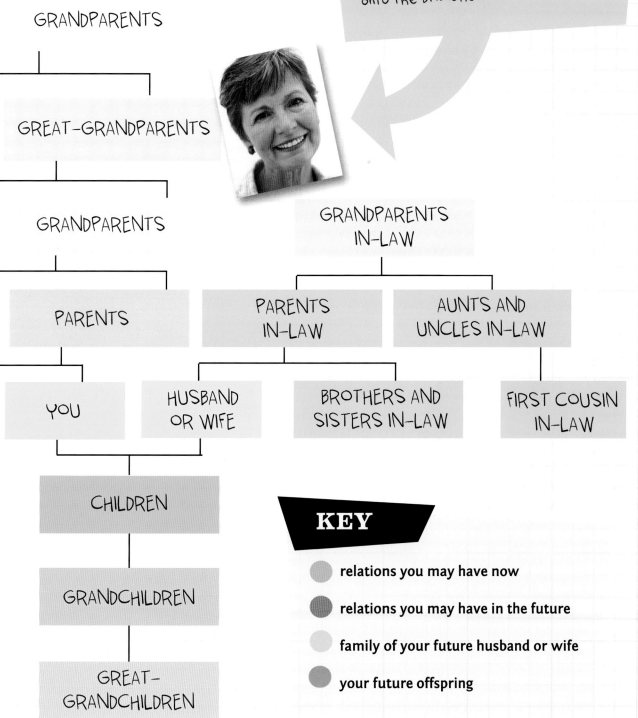

Try creating your
FAMILY TREE
Make it personal by taking photos at a family gathering and sticking them onto the branches.

GRANDPARENTS

GREAT-GRANDPARENTS

GRANDPARENTS

GRANDPARENTS IN-LAW

PARENTS

PARENTS IN-LAW

AUNTS AND UNCLES IN-LAW

YOU

HUSBAND OR WIFE

BROTHERS AND SISTERS IN-LAW

FIRST COUSIN IN-LAW

CHILDREN

GRANDCHILDREN

GREAT-GRANDCHILDREN

KEY

- relations you may have now
- relations you may have in the future
- family of your future husband or wife
- your future offspring

HOW CAN I BE SURE I AM RELATED TO MY FAMILY?

Looking at your *ancestors* in an album or on video can give you a great sense of your place in a big family clan. But matching faces doesn't really prove a family relationship. Even official records aren't always right. Fortunately, there is an absolutely certain way of checking up on ancestors.

Could Mom have accidentally swapped me at the hospital?

But doesn't *DNA* have billions of parts? How can you test them all?

But you told me that all humans share almost all the same genes!

So how would they prove that you're really my father?

How close can they be?

Where do the DNA samples come from?

So why wouldn't they be willing? Or living?!

So I could dig up a long dead ancestor and prove I was related to them?

Countless traditional stories begin with moms accidentally swapping newborn babies. Today, newborns get plastic wrist tags that stop this happening. If there is any doubt, we can prove who's mom and who's dad by testing their *DNA*.

You don't need to test them all. Just comparing short sections of the DNA "rope" reveals a family relationship.

True, but genes make up only two in every hundred parts of human DNA. The rest is known as "junk DNA," and it varies a lot between individuals. It's these stretches of DNA that can identify people.

By showing up repeated patterns in the order of base pairs in the strand of *DNA*. Unrelated people are very, very unlikely to have the same repeated patterns at the same point on a DNA strand. But in the DNA of relations, the repeated patterns are very, very alike.

In identical twins, all the repeated patterns appear at exactly the same points. A child's patterns will match about half the patterns of a parent (because children get half of their DNA from each parent). More distant relations share fewer patterns. The patterns of complete strangers won't match at all.

If you are testing two willing, living people, you would probably collect DNA by wiping the insides of their cheeks.

DNA testing is used to solve crimes by identifying victims (who may be dead) or suspects (who may not want to give a DNA sample).

Exactly! In 2008, German scientists did a DNA test on 3,000-year-old bones found in a cave. They found a match in the DNA of two men living nearby. The men were direct descendants of the dead caveman. He was their (deep breath) great-great-great-great-great-great-great-great—plus another one hundred greats—grandfather!

HOW WILL I CHANGE AS I GROW?

There's much more to growth than a row of pencil marks on the edge of a door. As we get older, our brains change almost as fast as our bodies. We get smarter, wiser, and more able to cope with the stuff—good and bad—that life throws at us. And when we stop getting taller, our brains still have a way to go.

YOU MUST BE KIDDING!

Leaving childhood behind at *puberty* is one of life's biggest steps. As we become teenagers, our bodies change in obvious ways. But sprouting hair in new places is only half of the story. There are more subtle physical changes, too. They make men and women appear different, even when seen fully dressed from behind. Boys become more angular and muscular as they grow up, while girls' bodies become more rounded.

OH, GROW UP!

Brain scientists have described the teenage brain as "work in progress." The *limbic system* that rules our *emotions* is still developing at this time of life—and quickly. The front of the brain—which controls reasoning and making sensible decisions—just can't keep up. No wonder our parents have such a hard time coping with our moods and desires when we're in our teens.

GROW SLOW

Our physical growth virtually comes to a halt when we hit 20 or so, but a few parts, such as our ears, carry on growing all our lives. If Methuselah, the Bible's oldest man, really had lived to celebrate his 969th birthday, his ears would have grown so big that they would have kept his head dry in a shower.

TRAIN THAT BRAIN

Does age really make you wiser? Well, up to a point. Our brains are at their fastest around 25 years of age. After that, we soon become less quick-thinking. However, other brain skills don't wind down or stop altogether. If we carry on learning all our lives, we can actually add to our wisdom and *knowledge* right into our 70s.

HOW AGE CHANGES US

Plotting our abilities as graphs shows how they rise and then decline as we age. However, growing *knowledge* makes up for reduced power. An old man who knows how to use a lever can lift a heavier weight than a young man using muscle strength alone.

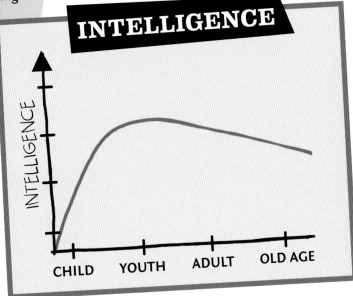

INTELLIGENCE

INTELLIGENCE

CHILD   YOUTH   ADULT   OLD AGE

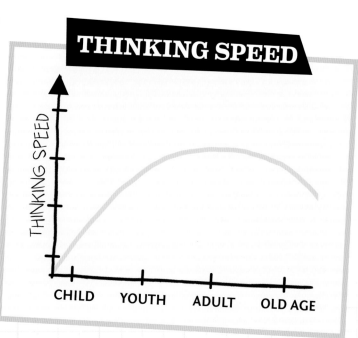

THINKING SPEED

THINKING SPEED

CHILD   YOUTH   ADULT   OLD AGE

STRENGTH

STRENGTH

CHILD   YOUTH   ADULT   OLD AGE

HEIGHT

HEIGHT

CHILD   YOUTH   ADULT   OLD AGE

WHAT MAKES MY BODY GROW AND CHANGE?

Surging and swirling from glands scattered around your body, *hormones* are chemical messengers. It's hormones that control how fast you grow, and how your body alters as you become an adult. These changes are slow, but hormones can also act at lightning speed, too. It's a hormone—*adrenaline*—that suddenly sets your pulse racing when you are scared.

Q **WHICH HORMONE MAKES ME TALLER?**

A This one is easy to remember! It's called human growth *hormone* (HGH). During childhood, the pituitary gland at the base of your brain produces a trickle of HGH, triggering your body to grow (see also page 130).

Q **DO HORMONES EVER STOP WORKING?**

A In middle age, gender *hormones* slow up. This brings to an end a woman's ability to have children—a change called the menopause. For men, the drop in hormone levels causes less dramatic changes, but can lead to strange behavior such as buying a powerful car, or even joining a rock band!

Q SO WHY ARE KIDS IN THE SAME CLASS OFTEN SO DIFFERENT IN SIZE?

A As children become teenagers, growth speeds up under the control of other *hormones*. These are called gender hormones, because their main task is to trigger the body changes that turn boys into men and girls into women at *puberty*. But the age at which gender hormones kick in is not fixed—so some kids race ahead, while others develop later.

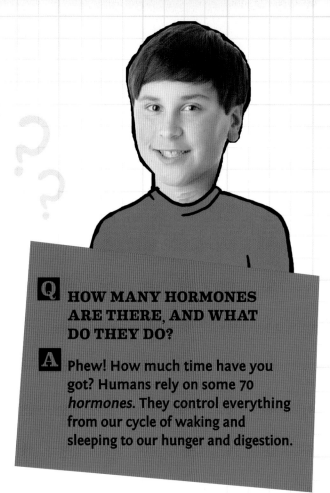

Q HOW MANY HORMONES ARE THERE, AND WHAT DO THEY DO?

A Phew! How much time have you got? Humans rely on some 70 *hormones*. They control everything from our cycle of waking and sleeping to our hunger and digestion.

Q WHAT MAKES A HORMONE WORK?

A The *gland* that makes a *hormone* also keeps track of the amount of it that is circulating in your blood, producing more when the level drops off and shutting off when too much is produced. Parts of the brain also control some hormones. For example, fear makes the *hypothalamus* send a signal to the adrenal glands to produce *adrenaline*, the "fight or flight" hormone.

WHERE DO HORMONES COME FROM?

They come from *glands*, special organs in the body. Some of the most important glands are shown below, but other major body organs also produce *hormones*.

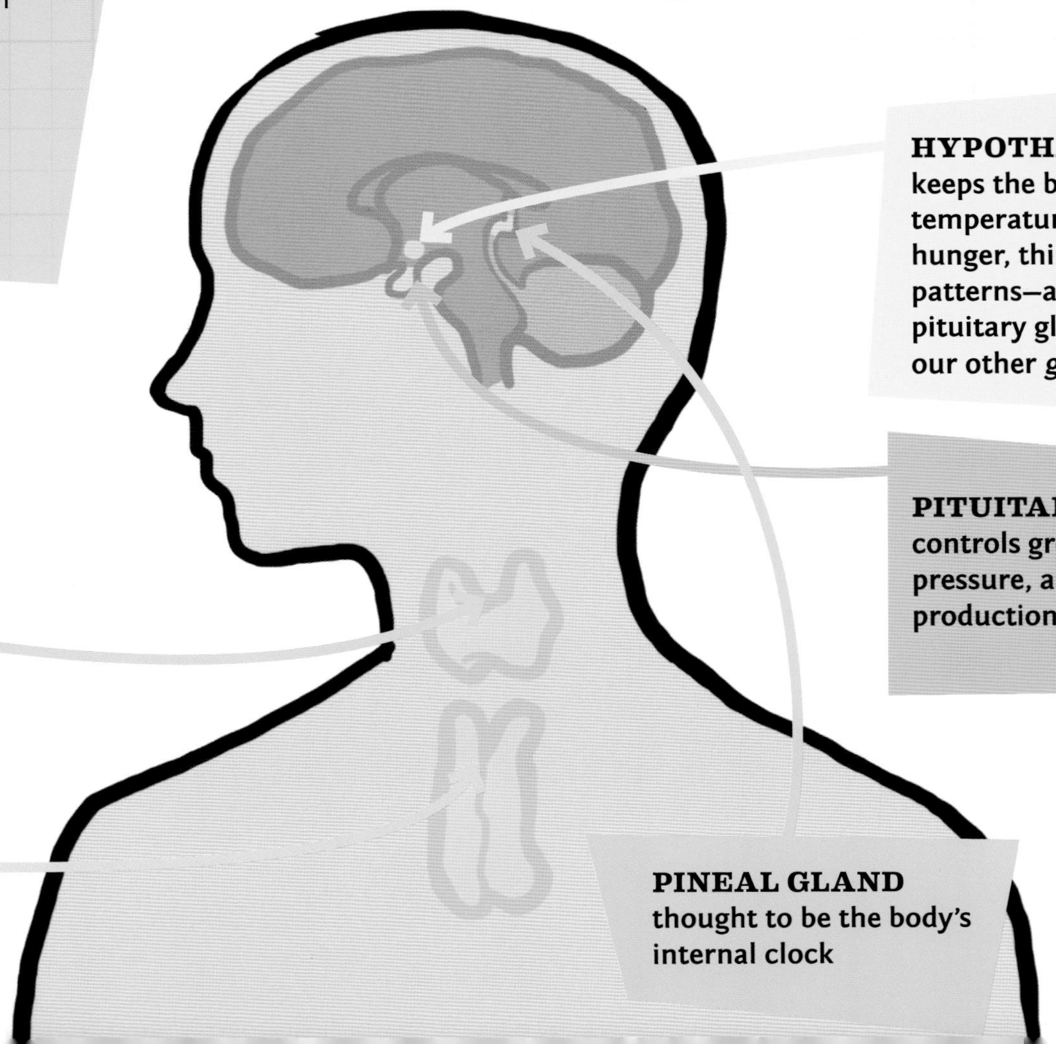

HYPOTHALAMUS keeps the body at the right temperature, controls our hunger, thirst, and sleep patterns—and, with the pituitary gland, regulates our other glands

PITUITARY GLAND controls growth, blood pressure, and urine production

PINEAL GLAND thought to be the body's internal clock

THYROID GLAND controls how the body grows and uses energy

THYMUS in childhood, teaches the body's infection-fighting white blood cells to identify harmful organisms

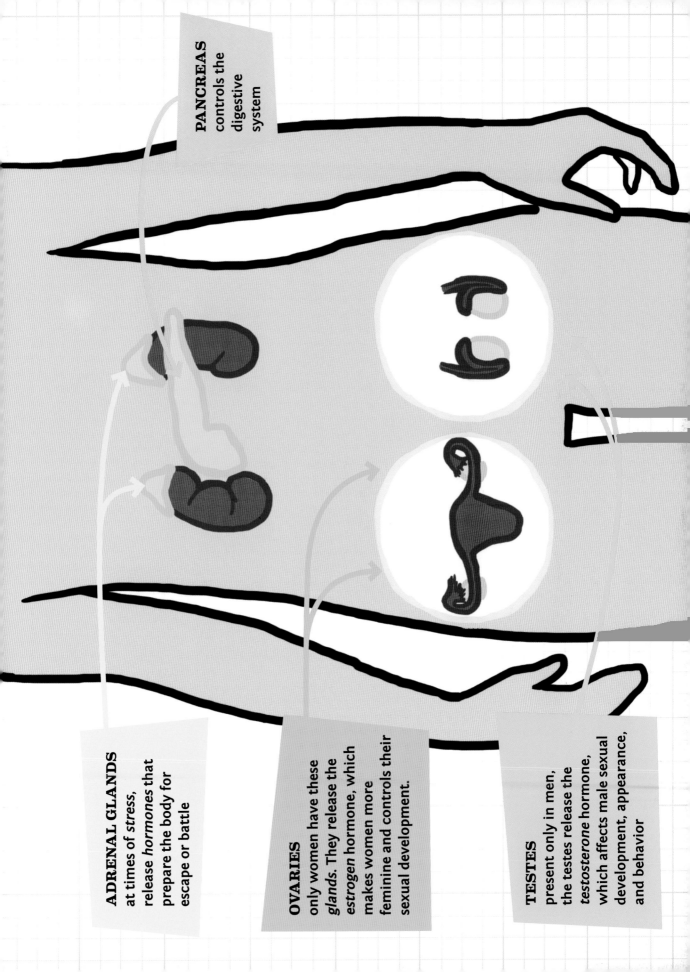

PANCREAS controls the digestive system

ADRENAL GLANDS at times of *stress*, release *hormones* that prepare the body for escape or battle

OVARIES only women have these *glands*. They release the *estrogen* hormone, which makes women more feminine and controls their sexual development.

TESTES present only in men, the testes release the *testosterone* hormone, which affects male sexual development, appearance, and behavior

WHAT HAPPENS IF I DON'T STOP GROWING?

Don't worry! You will. Sometimes it seems like your growth has gone into overdrive. You grow out of shoes and clothes long before you wear them out. It's not just an impression: for short periods kids grow nearly 2 millimeters taller each week! If this went on forever, we would all be as tall as trees! Fortunately, growth slows down.

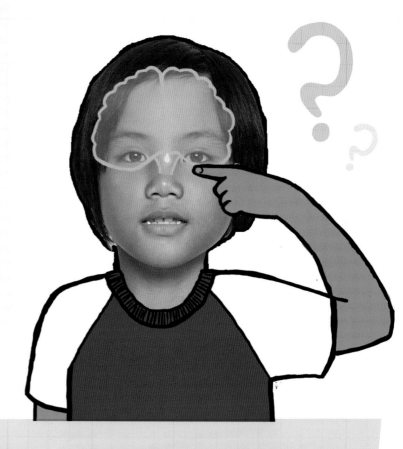

GROWTH GLAND
It's mainly the pituitary *gland* that controls your growth. The size of a pea, it nestles in a bony globe at the base of the brain. Your pituitary makes human growth *hormone* (HGH) that causes cells to grow and multiply, and in childhood it makes bones lengthen.

CONTROLLING THE CONTROLLER
How does the pituitary *gland* know how much growth *hormone* to release? It's controlled in turn by another hormone released by part of the brain called the *hypothalamus*. So really it's your brain that's in charge of stopping and starting your growth.

the pituitary gland

PLAYING CATCH-UP

Kids with pituitary glands that don't work hard enough won't grow fast enough. However, they can boost their height by having doctors inject doses of the *hormone*. (Athletes realized they could boost their muscles by doing the same thing, so there are now tests for checking at major competitions and in professional sports.)

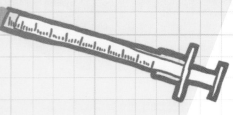

HANDS AND FEET FIRST

Nobody grows evenly. In the early teens, hands and feet get a head start on the rest of the body. Shin bones and forearms grow next. The spine is last to grow. No wonder teenagers feel gangly.

REAL-LIFE GIANTS

About three people in every million have a pituitary gland that makes too much growth *hormone*. Unless they receive medical treatment to control the gland, they grow into giants. This may give them an advantage in basketball, but it also leads to health problems and a shorter life.

Thanks to an overactive pituitary gland, U.S. basketball player Kenny George grew to 7.5 feet (2.3 m).

HOW LONG WILL I LIVE?

How long do you want to live? Just 200 years ago, the average *lifespan* was around 40, because so many babies died young and because medical care and sanitation were so poor. The average lifespan doubled in the 20th century in countries such as the U.S. and U.K., and today 100-candle birthday cakes are not so unusual. Until recently, everyone believed death was impossible to avoid. Now, though, not all scientists are so sure.

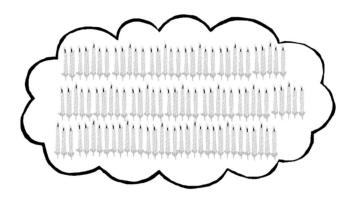

WHAT MAKES YOUR BODY AGE?

Your body's *cells* constantly renew themselves by splitting, making two cells where there was one before. However, they gradually lose this ability to divide. Without cell division, your body begins to decay, but this alone is not enough to end your life.

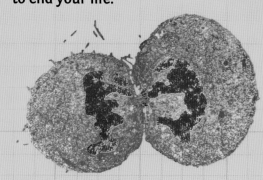

NOT THOSE GENES AGAIN!

We can never be entirely in control of how long we live. Scientists now know that there are "old-age" genes. Those of us who have them in our *DNA* will live longest. On the other hand, hardship damages our *genes*—and those of our children. If your grandmother suffered in a famine, for example, you are more likely to suffer from ill health such as heart disease.

DEADLY GERMS

Your life may be cut short if you catch an *infectious disease* and cannot get treatment. In the developing world, where few families have access to medical care, a lot of young people die this way. But their deaths could be avoided. Doctors can now prevent or cure many diseases that used to be deadly.

Thanks to *medicine* and better *diet*, we are all living longer: each day, the average *lifespan* increases by five hours. *Research* now suggests that it may soon be possible to live for 150 years.

EAT LESS, LIVE LONGER!

One promising way to increase your lifespan is to eat less, much less. Half-starved mice live twice as long as well-fed mice. It may work for humans, too, if they can put up with constant hunger.

No thanks. I'm much too full.

WATCH OUT FOR THAT CAR!

Want to celebrate your 30th birthday? Take the bus! Car crashes are the leading cause of death for people aged 10 to 24. Nearly a third of all boys and young men who die prematurely are involved in car accidents.

OR

TAKE CARE OF YOURSELF

In the western world, most old people die of heart disease, *stroke*, blocked arteries (blood tubes), or *cancer*. It's possible to avoid—or at least delay—these causes of death by living a healthy life. The people who live longest are not overweight, they exercise regularly, they don't smoke, and they don't eat junk food.

WHAT IF PARTS OF ME WEAR OUT?

Wouldn't it be great if we could *renew* body parts like we upgrade computers? Does your mom keep losing her car keys? "It's your memory, Mom—I'll order you a couple more gigabytes of RAM." This may sound far-fetched, but actually it's not. Researchers have wired up people's brain cells so they can control computers by thought alone. Scientists may soon be able to repair genes, too—a sort of software upgrade for our DNA.

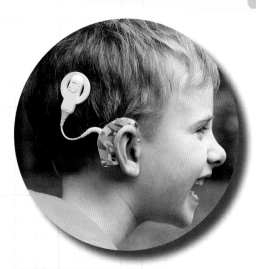

ROBO-ARM
By wiring up the brains of people who cannot move their *limbs*, scientists have made it possible for them to control a robot. They hope the same technology will make artificial legs and arms work more like the limbs they replace.

BIONIC EAR
More than 200,000 people already have computer-*enhanced* senses. Cochlear implants enable the deaf to hear sound. A microphone worn like a hearing aid picks up sounds and broadcasts them. The signal passes through the skull to the *implant* buried inside. This is wired in to the hearing nerve that runs to the brain.

HELPING THE BLIND TO SEE

Tiny video *chips* in the eyes of blind patients can replace the damaged retina. This layer of seeing *cells* normally sends vision signals to the brain when light falls on it. The current chips are 1000 times less sharp than the cheapest digital camera, but in tests users could still recognize everyday objects.

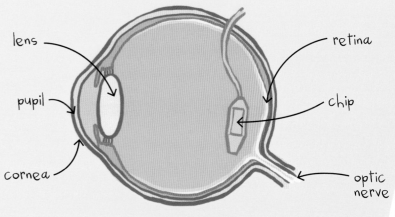

A human eyeball seen from the side.

lens
pupil
cornea
retina
chip
optic nerve

CHIPS WITH EVERYTHING

The *hippocampus* is essential for memory. So damage to it—through a *stroke* or Alzheimer's disease—leaves people unable to remember more than a few minutes of the past. Scientists have developed a "hippocampus on a chip," which works in rat brains. *Human* tests are still some way into the future.

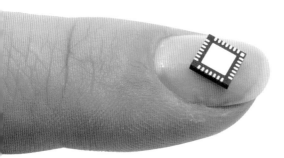

MENDING BROKEN GENES

Gene therapy aims to replace defective genes with normal *DNA*. To deliver the replacement genes, researchers use viruses. These tiny germs normally spread diseases by tricking our bodies into making more and more of the virus. But loaded up with the good DNA, the virus is hijacked, spreading the gene repair to where it's needed instead.

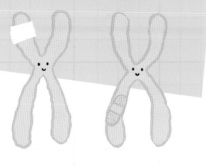

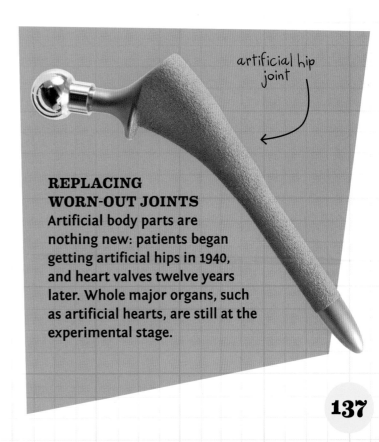

artificial hip joint

REPLACING WORN-OUT JOINTS

Artificial body parts are nothing new: patients began getting artificial hips in 1940, and heart valves twelve years later. Whole major organs, such as artificial hearts, are still at the experimental stage.

HOW MUCH OF ME WILL SURVIVE BEYOND MY LIFETIME?

Imagine you are a scientist of the 26th century. How much could you find out about the real YOU of the 21st? You wouldn't have much to go on. After five centuries, few of us amount to more than a pile of bones. However, you might be amazed at what these reveal. Even today, archaeologists and forensic scientists are expert at making bones tell their story. 500 years from now, they will be able to discover even more.

MY MONEY
Coins show the earliest possible date at which your life ended.

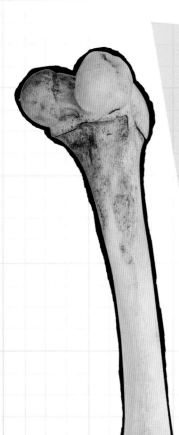

MY BONES
There's lots to learn from a pile of bones:
- Their size and hardness can show your age and height.
- The shape of your hip bone shows if you were male or female.
- Your skull shape hints at your race.
- Jagged damage suggests a violent death.
- A bent spine could result from hunching over a keyboard or console.
- A few diseases, including tuberculosis, gout, arthritis, and leprosy leave traces in the bones.

Bones get bigger where strong muscles attach to them, so bones can also show:
- whether you were fit or a couch-potato;
- whether you were left- or right-handed;
- what work you did; and perhaps
- even how much time you spent sending text messages!

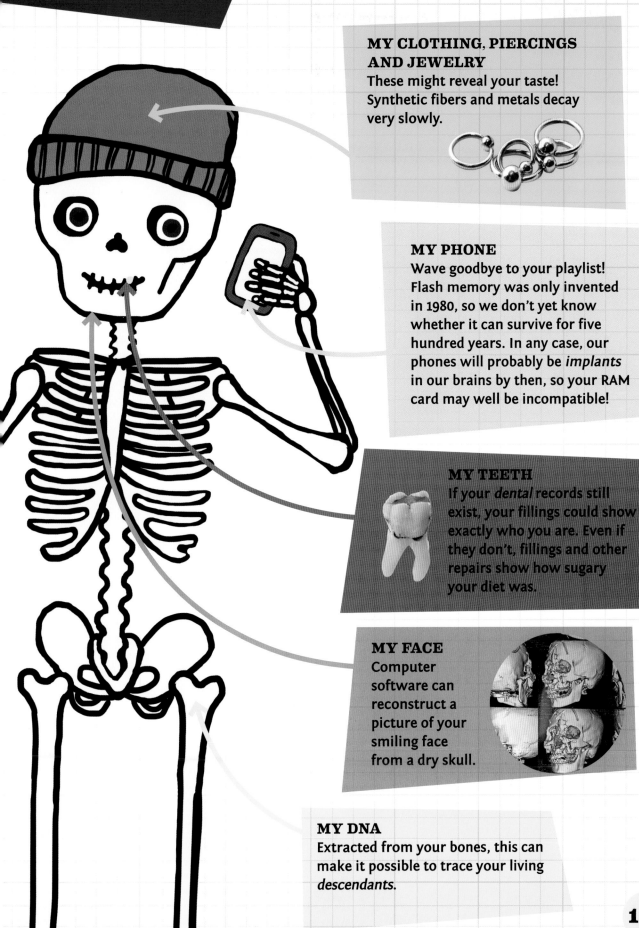

MY CLOTHING, PIERCINGS AND JEWELRY
These might reveal your taste! Synthetic fibers and metals decay very slowly.

MY PHONE
Wave goodbye to your playlist! Flash memory was only invented in 1980, so we don't yet know whether it can survive for five hundred years. In any case, our phones will probably be *implants* in our brains by then, so your RAM card may well be incompatible!

MY TEETH
If your *dental* records still exist, your fillings could show exactly who you are. Even if they don't, fillings and other repairs show how sugary your diet was.

MY FACE
Computer software can reconstruct a picture of your smiling face from a dry skull.

MY DNA
Extracted from your bones, this can make it possible to trace your living *descendants*.

What does "phobia" mean?

Check the glossary below

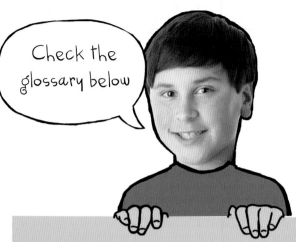

A

adapt To change, improve, or develop something when needed. 27, 42

adrenaline A hormone produced by the adrenal gland and released into the body through fear or anger. 88, 102, 126, 129

amnesia Loss of memory. 64–67

amygdala Part of the brain that processes emotions, and helps react to threats and danger. 49, 63, 91–92

ancestors Someone's parents or, more often, their grandparents or great-grandparents, and so on, right back to the first humans. 77, 90, 112–121

artery A tube that carries blood all over the body from the heart. 24, 92

average The usual or the most common size, number, or amount. 31

B

base pair A combination of two simple chemicals that makes up the smallest part of a DNA strand. 12

bionic Combining the body parts or abilities of a human and a robot. 27, 136

blush To turn red in the face. 88

C

cancer A disease in which affected cells increase in number and spread more quickly than normal, threatening health. 135

cell The smallest, most basic structure of a living thing. 12–15, 18, 72, 132

cerebellum Part of the brain that is in charge of the timing and exact control of body movements. 81

cerebrum The main, top section of the brain where most of our thinking goes on. 38,

chip A miniaturized circuit for processing data inside a computer. 137

chromosome A long piece of coiled DNA containing many genes. 13–15, 18, 104

circadian rhythm The repeated brain and body activity that follows a daily, 24-hour pattern. 46

clone To make a copy of a living thing with exactly the same genes. 13

cosmetic surgeon A doctor who changes a patient's body or face to make the patient feel prettier. 53

 D

dental To do with the teeth. 139

descendants Someone's children, grandchildren, great-grandchildren, and so on. 112–113, 121, 139

diet The things that you eat. 17, 31

DNA A twisted ladderlike chemical with its billions of parts arranged in a sequence that's unique to you. 12–15, 112–113, 120–121

dopamine A natural "happy chemical" released in the brain during pleasure. 96, 101

 E

EEG (Electroencephalograph) A scientific machine that measures and charts brain activity. 47

egg A special female sex cell that grows into a baby when a man's sperm cell merges with it. 13, 18, 104

emotion A powerful feeling or mood, resulting from our experiences or surroundings, which is hard to control with thinking or knowledge. 88–103 (also 35, 49, 51, 63)

enhance To make better. 136

environment Surroundings and living conditions. 17

estrogen A gender hormone that controls women's growth and development, and how feminine they are. 55, 129

evolve To gradually change and develop with each generation of a living thing. Plants or animals that are better in some way than their brothers and sisters are more likely to survive, and thus pass on the improvement to their offspring. 112–113

 F

frontal lobes The front part of the brain that thinks about the future, that spots similar things, and that helps remember emotions. 49, 96

 G

gender The sex—male or female—of an animal. 104–111

gene The biological "plans" that tell our bodies how to develop and grow. 12–23

gene therapy A medical method for introducing new or changed genes into the body to repair damaged or incorrect genes. 137

generation People in a family who are around the same age and are the same number of steps down from an ancestor. 19, 118

genetic disorder A disease caused by a fault in the genes that someone can pass on to their children. 20

gesture A movement of the body that is used to send a message. 84–87, 89

gland An organ in the body that produces hormones or other substances needed by the body. 128–129

gut reaction Doing something quickly because of an emotion rather than for a carefully thought-out reason. 89

 H

hippocampus Part of the brain that helps in dealing with emotions and in making lasting memories. 57, 63, 137

horizon The distant line where the sky meets the sea or land. 75

hormone A signaling chemical that moves around the body in fluids such as blood. 126–129 (also 55, 92, 105, 108)

puberty The physical changes by which a child's body becomes an adult body. 105, 122, 127

pupil The small circular window in the middle of the eye through which light enters. 72, 93

race A group of people who have the same skin color and appearance, and who often share traditions and beliefs. 112

random In an order decided by chance rather than carefully arranged. 18

red blood cells Saucer-shaped cells that carry oxygen around the body in the blood. 93

REM sleep Short for rapid-eye-movement sleep: a phase of dreaming sleep in which the sleeper's eyes moves quickly. 44

renew To replace. 136

rhythmic Having an obvious, regular, repeated beat. 73

scan To pass a narrow beam of energy across or through something, recording a picture of its surface or inside. 39, 40, 106

sense organ A special organ; such as the eye or ear, which gives us the ability to gather information about what's around us. 36, 44, 70–73

species A group of animals or plants sharing many similarities that together make them clearly different from other plants or animals. 55

sperm A special male gender cell that combines with a woman's egg to make a baby. 18, 104–105

stress Bad feelings or emotions that happen when someone must do more than they feel able to do or from experiencing unpleasant things. 129

stroke A sudden loss of the blood supply to part of the brain, making the sufferer unconscious, and often causing permanent brain damage. 66, 135, 137

symmetrical Having two sides that are alike, as if reflected in a mirror. 54

sympathize To tell someone that you understand how they feel. 110

testosterone A gender hormone that controls how men grow and develop, and how masculine they are. 55, 129

texture A pattern of higher and lower points on a surface, which you can feel by touching, or by shining light across the surface. 71

thyroid An organ in the neck that produces the hormones controlling growth and energy use. 128

tumor An abnormal growth in the body, especially one caused by cancer. 66

twins Brothers or sisters—often identical—born at the same time. 13, 23, 94

variant A kind or variety. 16

vein One of the tubes that carry blood back from all parts of the body to the heart, which pumps it around again. 24

vigorous Active, athletic, and full of energy. 31

Platt, Richard,
author.

The ultimate book
about me.

$14.99

DATE			